# BIG
# STYLE
— IN —
# SMALL
# SPACES

Easy DIY Projects to Add
Designer Details to Your Apartment,
Condo or Urban Home

## SARAH DORSEY
Founder of Dorsey Designs

PAGE STREET
PUBLISHING CO.

**PAGE STREET**
PUBLISHING CO.

First published in 2019 by
Page Street Publishing Co.

27 Congress Street, Suite 105
Salem, MA 01970
www.pagestreetpublishing.com

Distributed by Macmillan, sales in Canada by The Canadian Manda Group.

23  22  21  20  19    1  2  3  4  5

ISBN-13: 978-1-62414-788-3
ISBN-10: 1-62414-788-7

Library of Congress Control Number: 2018961068

Cover and book design by Meg Baskis for Page Street Publishing Co.
Photography by Sarah Dorsey

Printed and bound in China

# DEDICATION

To David and John. David, you're the other half of this book, and it's a reality because of your support, patience, dedication, creativity and ingenuity. John, always dream big and stay true to yourself—we love you.

# CONTENTS

THE
DORSEYS
EST.
2009

# INTRODUCTION

Hi friends, and welcome to our home! Small spaces and DIY have been a passion of mine and my husband, David, since we started renting about ten years ago. When we moved to California, we found ourselves renting again and, tired of our home lacking personalization, we started creating DIY projects and sharing them with readers on our blog, Dorsey Designs (www.dorseydesigns.com). Even though our space was small, it was full of personality. Our passion for creating was ignited!

David and I met about twenty-three years ago and have been together for about seventeen years. Early on in our relationship, David was interested in architecture, design and construction and I was interested in art and interior design, so our interests combined perfectly for DIY and home renovation. David is able to figure out my crazy ideas and make them a reality.

Small-space design is all about incorporating multifunctional, smaller-scale pieces and smart organization. You'll find projects throughout this book to help you achieve these things while also creating big style—whether it's a functional piece turned beautiful that you can display instead of storing or objects that transition well from space to space. I've also included "Get Organized" tips at the beginning of each chapter, in which I share my top pointers for making the most of your smaller space.

You'll notice that a number of projects involve wood. If you don't have a saw, don't let that scare you. We've always had one or two saws (e.g., a jigsaw is a great multipurpose compact saw), but we understand that not everyone can do that. All wood-related projects include an option to either have it cut for you or to use a hand-tool method.

David and I typically create large-scale, time-intensive projects. But, when developing this book, we wanted to create projects that were innovative and exciting yet achievable in a few hours or a weekend. We believe that just because a space is smaller doesn't mean that it has to sacrifice style. These projects have big style, yet are ideal for smaller spaces and achievable for weekend warriors like ourselves. I hope you enjoy!

# GETTING STARTED

Before you get started, think about how much space you'll need to complete a project. Each project has been labeled by workspace size. These are general guidelines to give you an idea of how much space is ideal for each project; but keep in mind that they are definitely flexible. You'll see a range of three space sizes:

1. Small: 6 x 6 feet (1.8 x 1.8 m)

2. Medium: 8 x 8 feet (2.4 x 2.4 m)

3. Large: 9 x 12 feet (2.7 x 3.6 m)

Projects have also been labeled by the average time required to complete them (i.e., a few hours, a day or a weekend). These times are variable, depending on your knowledge of the subject.

To make the most out of your project time, plan your weekend projects during the week and purchase your materials on a weekday night (stores are typically less busy on weeknights). That way you'll be ready to go first thing Saturday morning! Note that project time labels don't include the time needed to gather materials.

Protect your space. A lot of you will most likely be working in your main living space, so it will be important to protect your floors, furniture and textiles. Purchase canvas drop cloths from the home improvement store to place on the floor and over furniture. These fold easily and are reusable. Alternatively, use old sheets or tablecloths. Clear plastic also works; however, it typically doesn't last long, so you will most likely need to purchase more when tears develop. When applicable, tape edges or corners down with painter's tape to help keep the protectant in place.

# TIPS AND TRICKS

In the sections that follow, I've compiled a list of my favorite tips and tricks that I've learned along the way. These tips are my tried-and-true methods to ensure great results while making projects easier. You don't need to be a pro to DIY—with some tips and a little practice, you'll learn along the way!

## USING AN X-ACTO® KNIFE

For clean cuts, use an X-ACTO brand knife. Select one with number 11 blades. You will also need metal rulers with a cork back—6-inch (15-cm), 18-inch (45-cm) and 24-inch (60-cm) sizes are nice to have. If you select only one ruler, an 18-inch (45-cm) ruler is best. Finally, you'll need a self-healing gridded cutting mat, such as the 24 x 36–inch (60 x 90–cm) Alvin shown on page 16. I've had this since college and it has held up to a lot of cutting!

To get started, place your cutting mat on a flat surface, such as a countertop, table or floor. Set the material to be cut on the cutting mat, aligning the material on the mat's grid. Either use the grid to measure your desired cut, aligning the material to be cut on the grid or, from a straight edge of the surface to be cut, measure from two points, making a small mark with a pencil and aligning the ruler with those marks to create a straight line. Place your metal ruler on top of the surface, protecting the area that you will be using with the ruler. When you cut, do so on the opposite side of the ruler, away from the area you'll be using. If your cut strays from the ruler, the piece that you will be using will stay intact.

Place a sharp number 11 blade in the knife and tightly secure it. Place your nondominant hand on top of the metal ruler with your fingers clear of the edge of the ruler and the knife in your dominant hand. Start your cut by keeping your hand low—the blade should be fairly flat with the cutting mat, as you do not want to cut with just the tip of the knife. Drag the heel of your hand along the surface (this will help keep an even cut). It's important to cut slowly and to ensure as you go that your fingers are out of the way. Don't try to cut through the material in one pass. Making a few light, even passes is typically the best method. You'll know that it is time to change the blade when it doesn't cut as smoothly. Don't be afraid to change it frequently. This will make cutting much easier. I purchase blades online in packs of a hundred, to help with cost.

## PURCHASING CUSTOM-CUT WOOD

Get cleanly cut wood at the home improvement store. Explain to the associate what you are working on and ask if they can create even cuts. Ask to measure and mark the wood yourself (or observe as they mark). Ensure that the saw blade is on the outside of the pencil mark, so the area that you are using is the exact measurement needed. This will account for the thickness of the saw blade. For cuts that are exactly the same length, ask that the pieces are cut at the same time. Typically, home improvement stores will make a few cuts for free and charge for additional.

## HIRING HELP AND RENTING EQUIPMENT

For several cuts of wood, you can also hire a local carpenter. Locate some online and compare reviews. Also, if you feel comfortable with a saw, you can rent a saw at a local home improvement store and cut the items yourself. It's fairly inexpensive! A chop saw and jigsaw are great options for the projects in this book.

## SELECTING FINISHES

When selecting sealant and finishes, look for low- or zero–volatile organic compound (VOC) products if you are letting the items dry inside. Products will be labeled as such—cutting board oil is a good example. If you're using products such as polyurethane and stain, be sure to dry them outside until the product no longer off-gasses.

## KEEP YOUR SPACE ORGANIZED

Keep your tools and supplies in order while you work. Gather a few baskets to hold tools that you are using while working on a project. This is especially helpful when working on a project in your main living space over a few days—materials are easy to access, but your space stays tidy while you work. Bonus for lidded baskets that match your décor!

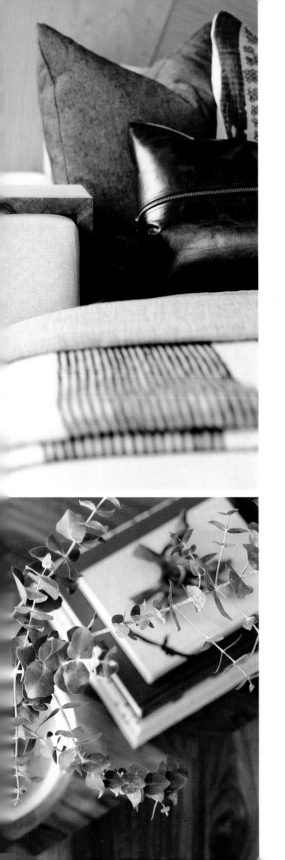

# LIVING

Typically, small-space living areas need to be multifunctional—they need to allow for relaxing, entertaining, playing and so on. But your living space should also be beautiful, since it's often the room that you're in the most and most likely open to the rest of your home.

This chapter is all about adding pretty DIY touches to your space, as well as DIY items that function well in smaller homes. I'll show you how to add concealed storage in an entertainment console to hide toys, electronic accessories and other items; an easy way to customize a solid pillow with leather; how to create a long picture ledge to display and easily change your art; and how to build a custom table from a countertop and premade legs.

## GET ORGANIZED

- Keep baskets around seating areas to quickly store everyday items. Bonus for lids to conceal items. This is also the perfect way to store tools for DIY projects.

- Unused corner? Add wall-mounted corner shelving to make the most of the space! Add a few rows to go from the floor to the ceiling and space them every 12 to 15 inches (30 to 38 cm).

- Need extra dining seating when you have guests over? Use accent chairs in your living room that can double as dining chairs when needed.

# FLOATING CONSOLE with Geometric Wood Doors

Time frame: 2 days | Workspace: Large

Creating a floating console out of kitchen cabinets is a smart way to get a streamlined storage piece that can be sized specifically for your space. Adding geometric wood veneer to the front takes it from basic to "Wow!"

When I was developing projects for this book, this project was one that I couldn't wait to try myself. The result was just what I had imagined in my head (love it when that happens). Read on to see how we built this custom floating console.

## MATERIALS

- 4 (15" x 18" [38 x 45–cm]) IKEA Haggerby flat-front cabinet doors
- 2' x 8' (60 x 240–cm) oak veneer with peel-and-stick back
- Pencils
- Yardstick or tape measure
- X-ACTO knife with #11 blades
- Self-healing cutting mat
- 2 (15" x 36" [38 x 91–cm]) IKEA Sektion flat-front cabinet bases
- ½" (13-mm) or ¾" (19-mm) plywood or 19½" x 76⅝" (48.75 x 191.5–cm) IKEA Forsand door (optional)
- 15" (38 cm) of ¾" (19-mm) white melamine edging
- Iron

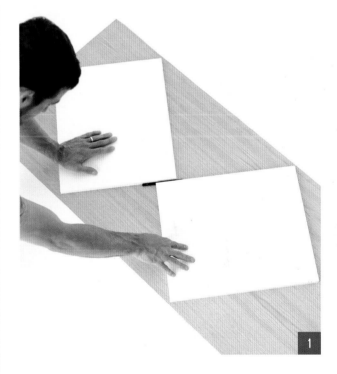

1. To create the wood grain pattern as shown, lay the first cabinet door horizontally on the veneer and turn the door clockwise until the upper right and lower left corners are even and parallel with the top of the veneer. Place the second door to the right with the long edge against the short edge of the first door. Place a pencil between the doors to create even spacing. Repeat this sequence for the second set of doors.

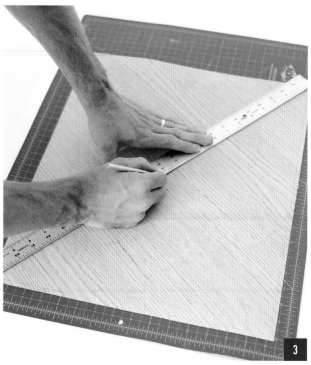

**2.** Once all of the doors are laid out, carefully trace around the edges using a pencil. Remove the doors and use the yardstick to trace a vertical line on the veneer connecting the top and bottom corners of the first and third doors and horizontal lines connecting the left and right corners of the second and fourth doors. Measure and lay out cut lines ¼ inch (6 mm) from the traced edges of the doors.

**3.** Using the X-ACTO knife, cut along the diagonal of the rectangle. One will be with the grain and the other will be against the grain.

**4.** Lay all the doors out and place the veneer as shown. Remove the backing gradually, starting at the center, and carefully align the corner of the veneer with the corner of the door. As you go, smooth the veneer down and gradually pull the paper back until the entire piece of veneer is attached. (Tip: It is helpful to have an extra set of hands for this step. The veneer isn't forgiving and should be applied correctly the first time.)

**5.** Repeat step 4, but this time place the contrasting grain veneer, carefully aligning the center edge. Repeat steps 4 and 5 for each door.

**6.** On a self-healing cutting mat, flip the first door over and carefully trim any excess veneer with the X-ACTO knife and #11 blade.

**7.** Attach the doors to the cabinet bases.

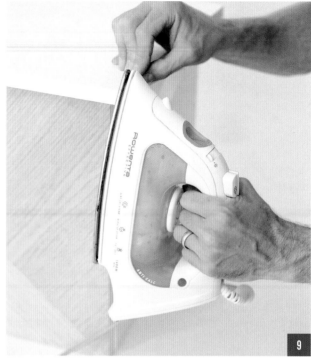

8. If desired, add a top to cover the top seam between the cabinets. Measure the entire console and cut the top to fit. (Note that an IKEA Forsand door was used for the console pictured after cutting its width and length to fit.) If you don't have access to a saw, the top can be cut at a home improvement store from ¾-inch (19-mm) birch plywood.

9. Finish the cut edge of the top by applying the white melamine edging with an iron on medium heat.

10. Trim any excess melamine edging on a self-healing cutting mat with an X-ACTO knife and #11 blade. Then attach it to the wall, following the cabinet manufacturer's instructions.

# QUICK CHEVRON COFFEE TABLE

Time frame: 1 hour | Workspace: Medium

One of my favorite projects from the early days of our blog is a wood herringbone coffee table. We lovingly milled and finished each piece of driftwood and built a coffee table top. It was time consuming to say the least!

We wanted to create a project that had the look without all the work! And we've done just that! Using a prefinished chevron wood countertop and adding legs creates high style with minimal effort.

I love a long table in front of the sofa. If space allows, make your table long and place lidded baskets underneath for extra storage—perfect for small spaces! Read on to see how we created this stunning, easy coffee table.

## MATERIALS

- 1 wood countertop (IKEA Barkaboda countertop, 74" [188 cm] shown)
- Ruler
- Pencil
- 4 (14" [35-cm] high) satin black hairpin leg, screws included
- Drill with 1/16" (2-mm) drill bit and Phillips bit

## PROJECT NOTE

Most wood countertops come in standard lengths, with all edges finished. If the size doesn't work for your space, it can also be cut to size with a table saw or circular saw. Wood countertops from IKEA come with a veneer strip that you can secure to the exposed edge if you decide to cut. Also, stores that sell custom countertops will be able to cut to size for you, if you don't have access to a saw.

1. To plan the placement of the legs, place the countertop on the floor with the bottom side up. From the short side of the countertop, measure in 6 inches (15 cm) and make a mark with a pencil. From the long side of the countertop, measure in 2 inches (5 cm) and mark. Repeat this on all remaining corners.

**2.** Where the 6-inch (15-cm) and 2-inch (5-cm) marks align, place the outer corner of the hairpin leg. The angle of the leg should flare out, as seen in the photo. Locate the hole on the bottom of the leg, and mark the location of the hole with a pencil on the countertop. Repeat on all remaining corners. Remove the legs.

**3.** On all marks created in step 2, predrill holes approximately the length of the screw with a ⅟₁₆-inch (2-mm) drill bit. Be careful to not drill through the entire countertop.

**4.** Place the hairpin leg, with the bottom of the leg flared out, on the countertop. Align it with the predrilled holes. Using the screws that were provided with the hairpin legs, secure the screws with a drill (a driver can also be used in this application). Repeat so all legs are secured. Flip your new table over and enjoy!

# LEATHER CIRCLE PILLOW

Time frame: 2 to 4 hours | Workspace: Small

Adding leather accents to a pillow might be easier than you think! Utilizing no-sew permanent adhesive and leather gives this a luxe look for less and can be completed in just an hour or so. The glue is permanent so, if needed, the pillow can be washed.

## MATERIALS

- 11½" (28.75-cm) diameter bowl
- 20" x 20" (50 x 50–cm) solid pillow sham with zipper (I got mine at H&M)
- 14" (35-cm) square piece of leather (such as from Leather Hide Store)
- Pen or pencil
- Scissors
- Sewing machine with natural thread (optional, if you would like a faux-stitched edge)
- Waterproof material (to be placed inside the pillow to prevent the glue from bleeding through)
- Ruler
- Masking or painter's tape
- Fabric and leather permanent glue

1.  Place the bowl on top of the pillow sham to determine the desired size of the leather circle.

2

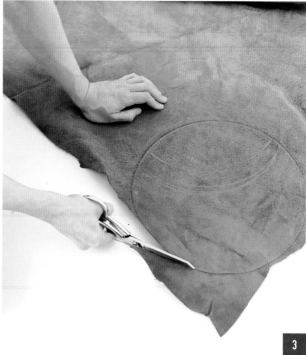

3

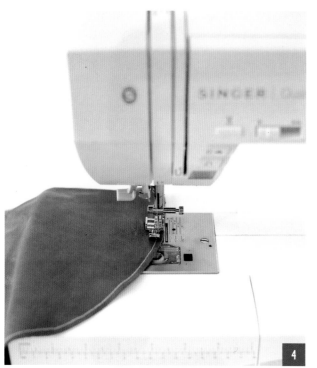

4

**2.** Place the bowl on the back side of the leather and trace around it with a pen or pencil.

**3.** Carefully cut along the line created in step 2 with sharp scissors. Go slowly, so that the cut is even.

**4.** You can create a stitch around the leather circle to make it appear as though it is sewn on the pillow. Using a narrow zipper foot as a guide, slowly sew around the entire circle so that there is a stitch around the perimeter. Contrasting, natural colored thread should be used. (Tip: Go slowly and stop very frequently to adjust the leather circle to keep a uniform line.) This step can be skipped if you do not have a sewing machine. You can also try hand-stitching if you prefer.

**5.** If your fabric is thin, place the waterproof material inside the pillow sham to prevent the glue from potentially bleeding through.

**6.** Place the pillow so the exterior is facing outward. Center the leather circle by measuring on all sides so that it is even.

**7.** As you measure, place small pieces of tape around the circle to reference later as you glue the circle down.

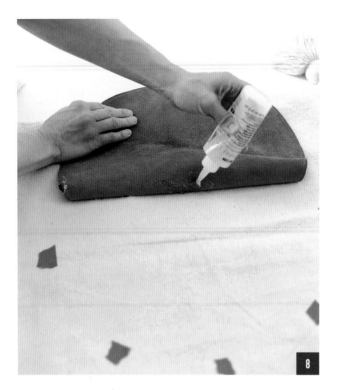

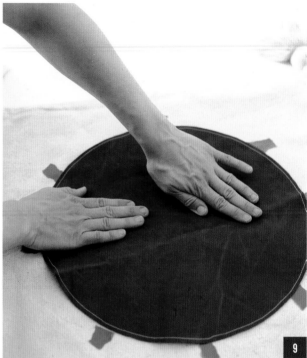

**8.** Starting at one edge, apply an even layer of permanent glue that is designed to work with both fabric and leather.

**9.** Hold down on the pillow sham to allow the adhesive to set and smooth out the glue as you go. Apply a little at a time and press smooth as the glue tends to dry quickly. (Tip: Be careful to not apply too much glue around the edge since it will be visible if it gaps out.)

# WOOD VENEER PHOTO MAT

Time frame: 2 to 4 hours | Workspace: Small

Photo mats add definition and elevate a photo or piece of art by creating visual separation between the image and frame. While they are optional, I typically include one to make a piece extra special.

Refresh an old mat or enhance a cheap, new mat by adding wood veneer to create interest and texture to your favorite frame. I used wood veneer left over from our Floating Console with Geometric Wood Doors (page 15) to create these geometric mats. This project will also work with one piece of veneer if you prefer a seamless look. It can be tailored to your preference.

Frames are perfect in smaller spaces because you can make a visual statement on a wall and not add to the footprint. Read on to see how to add texture to your plain mat!

## MATERIALS

- Photo mat (16" x 20" [40 x 50–cm] mat shown; select a frame with a mat in it, purchase a precut mat or cut your own)
- Peel-and-stick wood veneer (oak shown; be sure to purchase enough veneer to accommodate the square footage of the photo mat)
- Pencil
- Self-healing cutting mat
- 2 (18" [45-cm]) metal rulers with cork backs (or additional straight edge)
- X-ACTO knife with #11 blades
- Frame of choice (16" x 20" [40 x 50–cm] frame shown)

1. Lay the photo mat on top of the veneer. If you are using 1 piece of veneer for the entire mat, mark the four outer corners and four inner corners with a pencil. If you are using pieces to fill the mat, as shown here, trace all the inside and outside edges directly on the veneer with a pencil.

**2.** Lay the wood veneer traced in step 1 on the self-healing cutting mat. Align a ruler on the marks created in step 1 and trim the veneer with the X-ACTO knife fitted with a #11 blade.

**3.** Once the piece is cut out, remove a corner of the backing to reveal the sticky back.

**4.** Line up the corner and edges on the photo mat, slowly remove the backing as you go and secure the wood veneer on the photo mat. If your veneer doesn't match up perfectly, allow the excess or gap at the outer edge. This will typically be covered by the frame. If you are using 1 piece of veneer, this is the final step—you can insert the photo mat into the frame. Read on to see the remaining steps for multiple pieces of veneer.

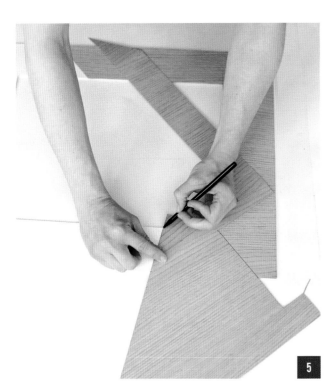

**5.** Once the first piece of veneer is secure, line up another piece of veneer on the back (keep the backing on). Mark all edges where the veneer meets the photo mat. Alternate the direction of the wood grain for a contrasting look.

**6.** Repeat steps 3 and 4 to secure the veneer to the photo mat. Then continue to fill the photo mat, repeating steps 2, 3, 4 and 5 until the photo mat is completely covered with wood veneer. As you trace, you may need to flip the photo mat and veneer over to mark edges as you go. If you can't see an edge to trace, on the veneer that is attached to the mat, align a ruler (or straight edge) with the edge of the veneer that you will be placing the additional veneer next to. Lay the veneer to be cut on top of the straight edge and line up the ruler with the straight edge below to draw a line. This will allow you to see the line below that you are matching and trace it accurately. Once complete, insert the mat into your frame.

# LONG OAK PICTURE LEDGE

Time frame: 2 to 4 hours | Workspace: Large

Displaying layered art is one of my favorite ways to fill the space above a sofa. It's highly customizable (i.e., perfect for those who change their minds frequently), and layering creates your own mini art gallery. Inspired by similar versions on Chris Loves Julia (www.chrislovesjulia.com) and The DIY Playbook (www.thediyplaybook.com), we decided to create our own version!

## MATERIALS

- 1 x 4 or 1 x 6 oak board (or similar wood; see Cut List)
- 1 x 2 oak board (or similar wood; see Cut List)
- Chop saw (optional)
- Level
- Tape measure or ruler
- Removable tape or pencil
- Stud finder
- Drill with ¼" (6-mm) paddle bit, ½" (13-mm) paddle bit and ⅛" (3-mm) bit
- Block of scrap wood
- 4¾" (12-cm) #14 screws (per stud spacing; 4 needed for a 10' [3-m] length)
- Masking or painter's tape
- 1¼" (3-cm) #6 brass screws (5 needed for a 10' [3-m] length)
- 220-grit sandpaper
- Sealant (optional; no sealer shown)

## CUT LIST

- Bottom of picture ledge: (1) 1 x 6 or 1 x 4 board, cut to length (e.g., 10' [3 m] for a 10' [3-m] sofa). A 1 x 4 board will allow two average frames to be layered. If space allows, a 1 x 6 board is recommended, as it will accommodate more frames. However, check that the depth will work for your space. You don't want it to extend too far if it is a narrow hallway or a heavy-traffic area.

- Facer board of picture ledge: (1) 1 x 2 board, cut to length (e.g., 10' [3 m] for 10' [3-m] sofa).

1. Cut the bottom of the picture ledge and the facer board of the picture ledge to length with a chop saw or have them cut at your local home improvement store. (See "Purchasing Custom-Cut Wood" on page 10.)

2. Determine the placement of the picture ledge on the wall. Use a level and measure, marking temporarily with removable tape (or pencil marks). (Note: The picture ledge shown is mounted 8 inches [20 cm] above the sofa. Locate the studs with a stud finder—typically, studs are 16 inches [40 cm] apart.)

3

4

5

**3.** On the bottom of the picture ledge, mark the stud's location, measured in step 2, on the center of the board.

**4.** On the bottom of the picture ledge, prepare to drill through the marks created in step 2 by finding the center of the board and creating an X. Using a drill fitted with a ¼-inch (6-mm) paddle bit, drill fully through the width of the board into a block of scrap wood.

**5.** Place a 4¾-inch (12-cm) #14 screw and ½-inch (1-cm) paddle bit on the bottom of the picture ledge to determine how deep you should drill. The thread of the screw should go completely into the stud. Mark this depth by placing a piece of tape on the bit to serve as a point of reference.

6

7

**6.** Using the ½-inch (13-mm) paddle bit, drill in the previously created ¼-inch (6-mm) holes to the depth found in step 5.

**7.** On the facer board, mark ⅜ inch (9.5 mm) from the bottom (this will enter the center of the bottom of the picture ledge where the pieces will eventually be joined) and 2 inches (5 cm) from each edge, with equal spacing between. For example, for a 10-foot (3-m) length, the remaining holes will be 29 inches (72.5 cm) apart.

**8.** Predrill the facer board with a ⅛-inch (3-mm) bit through the marks created in steps 6 and 7.

8

9

10

**9.** Line up the bottom board on the wall with the marks created in step 3. Attach the board to the wall with a 4¾-inch (12-cm) #14 screw so that the screw is completely in the board.

**10.** To attach the facer board, line up the bottom of the facer board with the bottom of the picture ledge and secure them together with 1¼-inch (3-cm) #6 brass screws through the holes created in step 8. With a 220-grit sanding block, lightly sand any rough edges. I left my picture ledge unfinished, but if you're painting your ledge, or adding a stain, apply sealant before use.

# CIRCLE SPLATTER ART

Time frame: 1 hour | Workspace: Small

Whether or not you consider yourself artistic, this splatter art is foolproof, affordable and looks great. Try creating a few versions—it's fun, fast and each version will be unique. Best of all, by cutting your own paper, you'll end up with several pieces that can be framed and customized.

## MATERIALS

- Picture frame with a paper insert (12½" x 12½" [31.25 x 31.25–cm] frame shown)
- Mixed media paper (at least 2 sheets the size of your frame or larger; I recommend a few extra sheets for practicing)
- Self-healing cutting mat
- Metal ruler with cork back (preferably 18" [45 cm])
- X-ACTO knife with #11 blades
- Bowl (for drawing template; I used a standard 7½" [18.75-cm] salad bowl)
- Pencil
- Lidded container to hold water and paint (I used a washed and dried yogurt container and lid)
- Acrylic craft paint (satin finish, any color) or any water-based paint (I've also had good luck with leftover interior wall paint; see project notes)
- Cardboard or drop cloth (to protect the work surface from splatter)
- 1" (2.5-cm) painter's tape
- 1" (2.5-cm) paintbrush
- Disposable gloves
- Paper towel

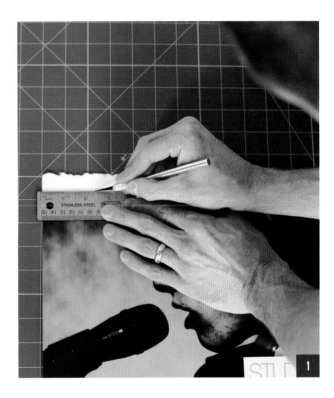

**1.** Remove the paper insert from the frame (you will use this as a template). Place one sheet of the mixed media paper on a self-healing cutting mat and place the paper insert on the edge of the mixed media paper. Using the metal ruler and X-ACTO knife, cut out an exact copy of the insert. Repeat this process with the second sheet of mixed media paper.

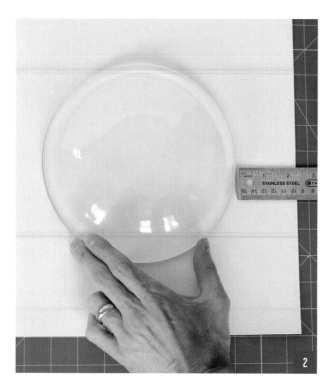

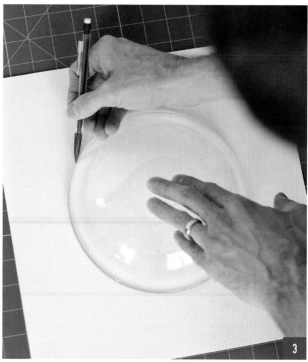

**2.** Center the bowl on one sheet of mixed media paper, using a ruler and measuring on all four sides to ensure that all sides are equal.

**3.** Once the bowl is centered, trace the outside perimeter with a pencil.

**4.** Cut out the circle. Following the pencil mark, carefully and slowly cut out the circle with the X-ACTO knife. (Tip: For thicker paper, such as mixed media paper, you don't have to cut through in one pass—you can make a few light passes. You have the most control of the X-ACTO knife if you hold the heel of your hand low and level with the paper, dragging the heel of your hand on the paper. This also helps prevent the blade from breaking.)

**5.** Prepare your paint. Fill up a small container with water and squirt a little paint into its lid.

**6.** Lay a sheet of mixed media paper, cut to the size of your frame, on a surface protected by a large piece of cardboard or a drop cloth. Lay the sheet of mixed media paper with the circle cut out on top. Tape the corners with painter's tape to keep the paper from shifting. (Tip: On a scrap piece of mixed media paper, practice splattering paint. Play with the thickness of paint by adding a little water to it—you want it thin enough to splatter but not so thin that it will run everywhere. Once splattered, the paint should be fairly opaque and not run fast. Do a few practice passes by flicking the paintbrush in horizontal and diagonal movements above the paper.)

7.1

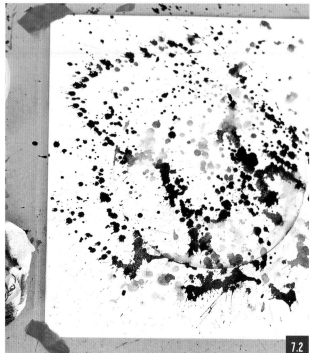

7.2

**7.** Next, start splattering your paper. Wear disposable gloves if you do not want to get paint on your hands. Keep a paper towel nearby to catch runny drips near the edge. Soak up excessive water by dipping a small piece of paper towel into the puddle to reduce big runs. Remove the tape and separate the 2 pieces of paper. Allow the splatter art to completely dry on a flat surface. As you get close to the edge of the circle, hold the paper down with your other hand to prevent the paint from running underneath. (A few runs are okay—they give the art a custom, handmade look. If you prefer fewer drips, add less water to the paint and use interior wall paint.) Repeat this process until the desired level of paint is achieved. I did two passes, one with a slightly thinner coat and one with a thicker paint to give it a little more depth. Splatter the extra circle cutout (leftover from cutting out the template) if you choose to frame it as well.

## PROJECT NOTES

· Craft paint will be a little runnier and create more imperfections and interior wall paint will be a little thicker.

· After completing this project, you'll have one square with a splatter circle, one square splatter piece with a circle cut out and one splattered circle (if you decided to use it). You can frame one or all of them!

· You can layer any color paper behind the square splatter piece with a circle cut out to make a complete piece. For the splatter circle, you can layer a square piece of paper (cut to the size of the frame) behind, center the circle and attach it with permanent double-sided tape.

· If your piece is wavy from the drying process, let it sit underneath a stack of books for several hours (preferably overnight) before framing. Once it's dry, insert it into the frame.

# SOFA ARM TABLE

Time frame: 2 to 4 hours | Workspace: Small

Short on space in your living room? If you don't have room for an end table next to your sofa, consider making your own sofa arm table. Requiring just a few simple cuts, this table is easy and quick to make. This table will work for any square sofa arm—perfect for holding your drink or snack while relaxing on the sofa!

## MATERIALS

- Tape measure and pencil
- 1 x 10 hardwood board (such as walnut, oak or maple)
- Chop saw (optional)
- Wood glue
- Clamps or painter's tape
- 220-grit sanding block
- Waterproof sealant (such as clear polyurethane)

1. Measure the width of your sofa arm—this will determine the width of the table. For the top of the table, take the width of the sofa arm and add the width of the sides multiplied by 2. For example, my sofa arm measures 5½ inches (13.75 cm) wide and the thickness of my wood is ¾ inch (19 mm), so the top of my table measures 7 inches (18 cm). Determine the desired side length (e.g., my sides measure 4 inches [10 cm] long). (Note: In the table pictured, the corners are mitered at 45-degree angles. To make this project even simpler, use straight cuts with the same measurements.)

2. Cut the top and sides from the hardwood. If you have a chop saw, use that or get your wood precut at the home improvement store.

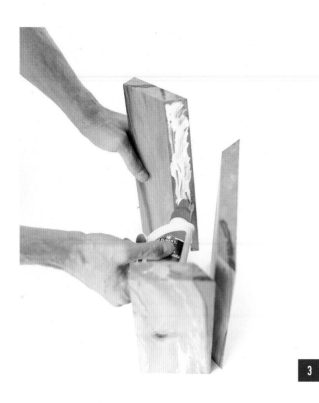

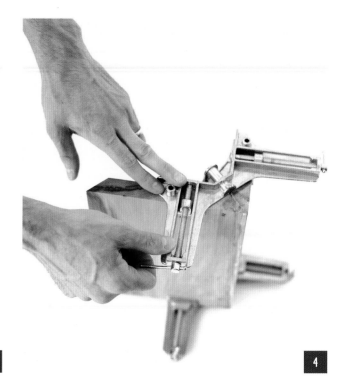

**3.** Once your cuts are made, apply wood glue on the edges.

**4.** Clamp or use painter's tape to hold the joints in place while the glue dries.

**5.** With a 220-grit sanding block, sand all the edges until smooth. If you plan to use beverages on the table, apply sealant to protect the wood from any moisture.

# ENTRY

Entries don't have to be large to make a great first impression. Utilizing vertical surfaces and narrow furniture that is multipurpose helps keep spaces organized and functional.

One of our first rentals had a tiny entry, but we made the most of it by placing a narrow, rounded table on a stair landing against the wall. With wall storage above and baskets below, all our daily items were easy to reach and organize.

In this chapter, you'll find a custom woven bench (perfect for putting your shoes on as well as storing your keys), custom art ideas and ways to make everyday items look luxe.

## GET ORGANIZED

- For vertical storage, create a built-in with narrow upper kitchen cabinets. Going floor-to-ceiling will give maximum storage! Or create a smaller floating cabinet with art or a mirror above for a more decorative look.

- Add wall hooks to your space to hang bags and coats. Stack them two high to maximize storage! Make a statement by adding wallpaper behind them or a vertical 1 x 6–foot (30 x 180–cm) tongue-and-groove wood board painted a deep color to add impact.

- No room for a bench or console? Utilize your wall space by securing narrow shelving, wall pockets or hooks, or even secure a fold-down bench to be used when you're putting your shoes on.

# COILED ROPE ART

Time frame: 2 to 4 hours | Workspace: Small

Inspired by one of my favorite designer pieces, this coiled rope art utilizes natural texture and materials. I love the simplicity of the piece, along with its interesting texture and contrasting materials.

This piece of art takes only a few hours to complete and adds instant warmth to your home. Even if you don't consider yourself artistic, this project makes it easy to achieve a stunning result.

## MATERIALS

- Square shadow box frame (20" x 20" [50 x 50–cm] shadow box shown)
- ¼" (6-mm) birch plywood, cut to size to fit in the shadow box frame (or wood veneer, for the no-saw method)
- Pencil
- Table saw or jigsaw (optional)
- Pre-stain
- Wood stain (Minwax® Wood Finish™ Jacobean oil-based stain shown; select a stain darker than the cord)
- Rag for applying stain
- Disposable gloves
- Yardstick
- Cord (hemp 180-lb [81.6-kg] test cord, approximately 150' [45 m], shown)
- Clear-drying fast-grab glue (Aleene's® Fast Grab Tacky Glue™ shown)
- Scissors

1. Prepare the wood backing. Remove the paper insert from the shadow box frame and place it on a square corner of the plywood. Trace the paper insert with a pencil and cut the plywood to size yourself with a table saw or jigsaw (or have it cut at your local home improvement store). If you prefer not to use power tools, use wood veneer and attach it to a substrate, such as a mat board.

**2.** Work in a well-ventilated space (preferably outside or in a garage). For an even finish, use a pre-stain prior to applying the wood stain, following the directions of the pre-stain's manufacturer. Apply the wood stain to the plywood with a rag as directed by the stain's manufacturer. Be sure to wear disposable gloves. (Note: Two coats of Minwax Jacobean are shown. If you don't have access to outdoor space, use a zero-VOC stain or leave the wood natural and use a darker rope to eliminate off-gassing inside.)

**3.** Find the center on the plywood by measuring the center of both diagonals with a yardstick and marking it with a pencil to create a small X. This will be the center for the coil.

**4.** Hold the cord between your thumb and pointer finger and start creating a coil. On the inside edge of the rope, secure the coil to the plywood with the fast-grab glue as you go. (I found it easier to start the coil loose and later transfer it to the plywood.)

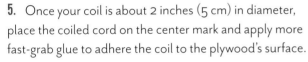

**5.** Once your coil is about 2 inches (5 cm) in diameter, place the coiled cord on the center mark and apply more fast-grab glue to adhere the coil to the plywood's surface.

**6.** Continue to work outward, applying glue evenly on the plywood's surface, and wrapping the cord to enlarge the coil. Carefully press down so that the coil adheres well to the plywood and doesn't bubble. Hold it in place while the glue sets.

**7.** Once the desired diameter is reached, cut the cord with scissors and glue the loose cord in place. (Note: A 10-inch [25-cm] diameter coil is shown.) After the glue is fully dry, insert the coil art into the shadow box frame.

THE DORSEYS EST. 2009

# WOOD VENEER WELCOME SIGN

Time frame: 2 to 4 hours | Workspace: Small

I've incorporated a welcome sign into most entries while renting. It adds personalization—perfect for both renters and homeowners alike! Utilizing warm wood veneer and contrasting matte black adds interest and character beyond a traditional black-and-white print.

## MATERIALS

- Front sheet of paper (black, 55-point 22" x 30" [55 x 75–cm] artist paper shown; see project note)
- Poster letters with adhesive backs (2½" [6.25-cm] shown; available at all arts and crafts stores)
- Yardstick
- Pencil
- 6" (15-cm) metal ruler with cork back
- X-ACTO knife with #11 blades
- Back sheet of paper (same size as front paper, any color)
- 4 (approximately 3" x 20" [7.5 x 50–cm]) pieces of wood veneer with peel-and-stick backing (or more as needed)
- Permanent glue for paper
- Frame (24" x 36" [60 x 90–cm] float frame shown)

1. Place the front sheet of paper on a work surface and lay out the poster letters to get a general idea of spacing. Align a yardstick vertically and horizontally to lay out the letters evenly. (Note: The spacing shown includes 2½-inch [6.25-cm] tall letters, starting 4 inches [10 cm] from the top and 2 inches [5 cm] from the left edge. There are 1½ inches [3.75 cm] between rows and ¼ inch [6 mm] between letters, with 4 inches [10 cm] above "2009". The cutout line between "est." and "2009" measures 17 x ¼ inches [42.5 x 0.6 cm].)

**2.** Once all the letters are level and spaced evenly, trace the outline of the letters with a pencil.

**3.** After all the letters and lines are traced, remove the poster letters. Use the metal ruler and X-ACTO knife to cut out the letters along the lines traced in step 2. Depending on the thickness of your paper, it may take a few light passes with the knife. Change the blade every few letters, as this will help create even cuts. Once your blade starts to drag some, you will know it's time to change it.

**4.** Place the front sheet of paper with the letters cut out on top of the back sheet of paper. With a pencil, make a mark on all exterior corners of each line. This will be the guide for the amount of wood veneer needed for underneath.

**5.** Referencing the marks created in step 4, cut out the wood veneer so it is large enough to completely cover the cutout letters. It doesn't need to be perfect, since the edges will be covered. Remove the backing from the veneer and place it on the back sheet of paper along the marks made in step 4.

**6.** Flip the front sheet of paper, with the letters cut out, and apply permanent glue for the paper on the back side.

**7.** Once the glue has been placed on the back of the front sheet of paper, place the front paper on top of the back sheet of paper with the veneer. The glue doesn't need to be applied extremely evenly, but try to apply it in one layer. It will even out when it is flat. Press down firmly until the glue sets.

**8.** Apply a little glue on the back of the center of any letters and apply where applicable. Ensure that no glue has seeped out and place a few heavy objects (such as books) on top of the entire piece to ensure that it dries evenly.

**9.** Once the piece is dry, frame it in the desired frame.

**PROJECT NOTE**

This thick paper was difficult to cut through—keep that in mind, especially if you have a lot of cuts. The added depth looks nice, but thinner poster-board thickness will also work.

# THE
# DORS
# EST.
# 2009

# WOVEN ROPE BENCH

Time frame: 1 day | Workspace: Small

Woven furniture has been popping up everywhere, and for good reason! It adds warmth and texture to spaces, pairing perfectly with upholstered pieces. Ideal for smaller spaces, benches can easily be used at an entry to put shoes on and moved to the dining table when extra seating is needed.

Using a premade slat bench provides a jump-start for this project. Requiring just a few materials, this project can easily be completed in a few evenings while relaxing and catching up on shows or chatting with friends.

## MATERIALS

- Bench with slat top (39⅝" [100-cm] IKEA Ypperlig bench shown)
- Rope (hemp 180-lb [81.6 kg] shown; approximately 620' [186 m] used; see project note)
- Gallon storage bag with closure
- Scissors

1. If needed, assemble the bench. Unravel the rope from inside the center of the coil. On the inside of the leg, wrap a loop around one slat of the bench, and tie tightly with two overhand knots.

**2.** Flatten the rope coil enough to thread it through the slat. Thread it through the slat, pulling all of the rope down.

**3.** Create a figure 8 pattern by bringing the rope over the other slat and back through the center, pulling all the rope down.

**4.** As you go, pull tight and push the rope tight in the center. (Tip: Place the flattened rope coil in the gallon storage bag to help keep it together as you thread it through the slats.)

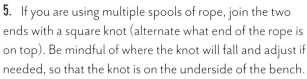

**5.** If you are using multiple spools of rope, join the two ends with a square knot (alternate what end of the rope is on top). Be mindful of where the knot will fall and adjust if needed, so that the knot is on the underside of the bench.

**6.** Repeat threading the rope in a figure 8 pattern until you've reached the inside of the other leg. Trim the rope with scissors, leaving about 1 foot (30 cm) of excess rope. Loop the rope back around one side and tightly tie two overhand knots. Cut off the excess rope.

**PROJECT NOTE**

If you are using multiple spools of rope, compare color before starting, as color may vary from spool to spool.

# OAK-FRAMED MIRROR

Time frame: 2 to 4 hours | Workspace: Medium

Thick wood mirrors have always been a favorite of mine. I've actually wanted a full-length mirror by the door for several years but never followed through since it didn't seem like a necessity. If you're wondering whether a large mirror is right for a small space—absolutely! There's no easier way to make a small space feel larger.

Using an existing thin frame, it's easy and inexpensive to add a wood surround to get a more substantial frame. This is a perfect DIY to get the look for less!

## MATERIALS

- Tape measure or ruler
- Framed mirror of choice (IKEA Hovet shown)
- Pencil
- 1 x 3 oak board (or comparable wood), cut into 2 (78¾" [1.96-m]) pieces and 2 (30³⁄₁₆" [75.5-cm]) pieces if using the IKEA Hovet mirror
- Chop saw (optional)
- Drill with ⅛" (3-mm) countersink bit
- 16 (1¼" [3-cm]) brass screws
- Wood glue

1. Measure your mirror to determine the wood cuts. The top and bottom cuts should be the width of the mirror, while the side cuts should be the height of the mirror, plus the width of the top and bottom cuts. In other words, the sides will be the height of the mirror, plus the thickness of the 2 pieces placed on the top and bottom. Cut the oak yourself or have it cut at your local home improvement store.

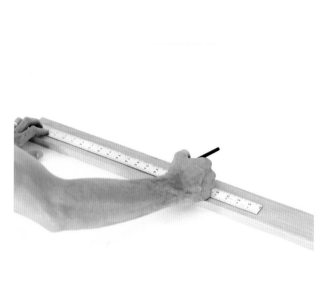

**2.** Place the mirror flat on the floor. On the top, bottom and two sides, measure the screw placement. Mark them with a pencil. Ensure that they are going into the center of the mirror frame behind the glass. If using the IKEA Hovet mirror, all screws are 1 to 1¼ inches (2.5 to 3 cm) from the back edge of the frame. The top and bottom holes are 2 inches (5 cm) from the ends, with 1 screw at the center (15¼ inches [38 cm] from the end). The sides are ⅜ inch (9.5 mm) and 16 inches (40 cm) from the end with 1 screw at the center (39⅜ inches [100 cm] from the end).

**3.** Using the drill fitted with the ⅛-inch (3-mm) countersink bit, drill through the wood so that the screw will sit flush with the exterior surface of the wood frame. Drill into a scrap piece of wood to protect the surface below.

**4.** Place the wood sides on the mirror. Starting with the top piece, hold on to the top of the frame and drill into the mirror frame through the holes created in step 3.

5

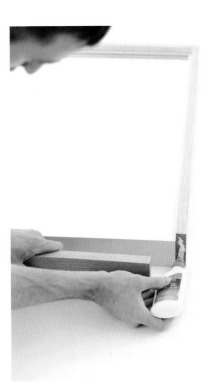

6

**5.** Insert the brass screws to secure the wood to the mirror frame. Repeat this process for the bottom of the frame.

**6.** Repeat steps 3 and 4 to secure the sides, but apply wood glue to the corner, where the wood meets, before inserting the brass screws.

# KITCHEN

When we moved into our home a few years ago, we knew that the kitchen would need a major renovation. It was small, dark, dysfunctional and easily our least favorite room. Today, it still has the same footprint, but we were able to reconfigure the space to maximize the function. Since renovating, it's light, bright, functional and a space that we love being in.

When we remodeled, we emptied our cabinets and purged everything that we didn't use, was broken or didn't bring us joy (mainly all the ugly things). To make the most of a smaller space, we ensured that each cabinet had a purpose, was organized and not overfilled. Along with renovating, a few personal DIY touches and some organization have transformed this space.

In this chapter, you'll find ideas for simple, impactful art, hardware hacks, textile projects and organization ideas utilizing some of my favorite materials and finishes. You most likely already have some of them!

Whether you've just renovated, are waiting to renovate or renting, these projects are perfect for your small space because they add both organization and aesthetics.

## GET ORGANIZED

- Keep everyday items corralled on the countertop by using a cutting board to group items. Place items—such as oil and vinegar in pretty jars, a salt cellar and a pepper grinder—on top.

- Add hooks to store small items such as tea towels and oven mitts inside cabinets. Just make sure that the thread of the hook is shorter than the depth of your cabinet face, to ensure that it doesn't poke through the front.

- Short on vertical storage? Inside a cabinet, use a plate rack to organize cookie sheets, food storage lids and cutting boards.

# POTATO STAMP TEA TOWEL

Time frame: 1 hour | Workspace: Small

Creating your own custom kitchen textiles is the perfect way to bring color and pattern into your space. Using a potato stamp makes this project completely customizable and affordable. Chances are you already have most of the materials in your home!

To consolidate storage, I like to keep a small basket under the sink to store towels when they are not in use.

## MATERIALS

- Drop cloth or plastic
- Ironing board and iron
- Natural-fabric tea towels (such as cotton or linen), prewashed and dried
- Potato (any variety; size and shape dependent on desired stamp)
- Sharp kitchen knife
- Water-based matte or satin craft paint
- Paint container for mixing
- Tintable fabric medium
- Paper towel
- 1" (2.5-cm) foam craft brush

1. Place a drop cloth or some plastic on your work surface to protect it from the paint. Then, on an ironing board and with the iron's steam setting on, lightly iron the prewashed tea towels. The ironing doesn't need to be perfect, just enough so that the stamp can be applied evenly.

**2.** Prepare the stamp by cutting the potato in half with a sharp kitchen knife. Ensure that the cut is straight—this will help keep the stamp even.

**3.** Next, cut the desired stamp design into the potato's flesh. For example, I cut thin lines across the stamp. For the negative space, I cut about ⅛ inch (3 mm) down in a V groove to easily remove the excess. Remember the area on the surface will be the stamp pattern and all excess removed will be the negative space in the pattern.

**4.** Prepare the water-based craft paint by using one color, or make your own by mixing two or more colors in a paint container. Next, add the tintable fabric medium, following the directions on the package.

**5.** Test the stamp by practicing on a paper towel. Using the foam brush, lightly apply a thin layer of paint to the stamp. Remove any excess paint with a paper towel—you want the paint to be light so it doesn't create globs. Lightly sweep across the stamp, starting at one end. Don't worry about getting the paint even—this will give it a handmade, one-of-a-kind look. Try out a few patterns by alternating the direction of the stamp.

**6.** Once you've practiced using the stamp and decided on the pattern, move on to the tea towel. Start on the bottom-left corner and work in rows, moving left to right. I alternated the direction of the stamp, vertically and horizontally. (Note: To keep variety in the stamp, I applied the stamp a few times before reapplying paint.) Working in rows, repeat this process until the entire towel is covered in stamps.

**7.** Once the paint has fully dried, follow the directions on the tintable fabric medium container for heat-setting the fabric so it is washable.

# LEATHER-WRAPPED CABINET HANDLE

Time frame: 2 to 4 hours | Workspace: Small

Looking to upgrade your handles without spending money on brand new hardware? Try wrapping your existing handles with leather! It's affordable and easy to do. Using leather and upholstery thread, this project is durable and stands up to daily use.

## MATERIALS

- Ruler
- Round or square cabinet handle
- Pencil
- 1 (4" x 4" [10 x 10–cm]) piece of leather per cabinet handle (leather from Leather Hide Store shown)
- Scissors
- Pen
- Leather punch or X-ACTO knife with #11 blades
- Upholstery thread (color of choice; natural shown)
- Thick upholstery needle

1. First, measure between the two connection points of your cabinet handle pull. This will be the width of your leather piece. To determine the length, measure around the pull—the four sides (if a square) or circumference (if round)—and add 1 inch (2.5 cm). This will be the amount needed to surround the pull (plus a little extra to be trimmed later; for my pulls, I needed a 3½-inch [8.75-cm] wide and 3½-inch [8.75-cm] long piece of leather).

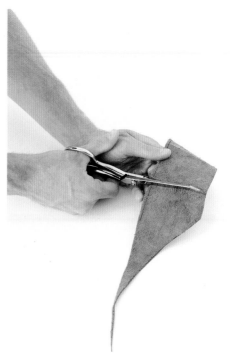

**2.** Using a ruler and pencil, measure and draw the dimensions from step 1 on the back of the leather.

**3.** Follow the lines created in step 2 and cut out the leather rectangle with scissors.

**4.** To lay out the holes for stitching the handle, measure and mark ½ inch (13 mm) from each of the leather's edges. Draw a line connecting the ½-inch (13-mm) marks on both edges. These lines will identify where the leather will meet once it's wrapped tightly around the handle.

**5.** On the line created in step 4, measure ¼-inch (6-mm) spacing and mark it with a pen. Repeat on the other line.

**6.** On the marks created on step 5, create a hole with a -inch leather punch. If you don't have a punch, you can create a small slit with an X-ACTO knife.

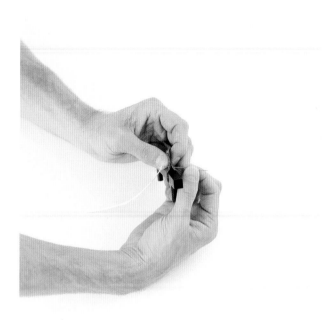

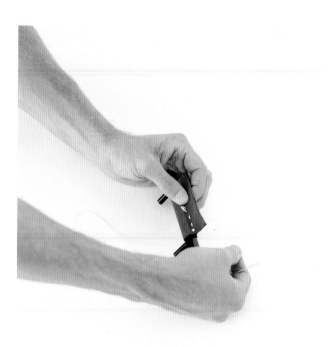

7

8

**7.** With the good side facing outward, wrap the leather around the pull and line up the holes created in step 6. Using scissors, cut a long piece of upholstery thread (about 2 feet [60 cm]). Thread the upholstery needle and knot the thread's ends together with a large knot so the thread won't slip through the existing hole.

**8.** Hand-stitch the leather, starting at one end, through the existing holes.

**9.** Once you get all the way across, go back and cover all of the alternating sections. This will create a solid stitch along the seam.

9

**10.** Once the stitches are complete, cut the excess thread, leaving a few inches, and create several knots to ensure that the stitching doesn't go through the last hole.

**11.** Carefully trim off the excess leather, cutting approximately ⅛ inch (3 mm) from the stitching. Alternatively, use a ruler and X-ACTO knife to create a perfectly straight line.

# WOODEN SPOON ART

Time frame: 2 to 4 hours | Workspace: Small

Cooking can often bring sentimental feelings of childhood memories. I love the idea of repurposing old wooden spoons, perhaps from a loved one, into art. I used wood veneer as a backing, but I also love the idea of using old recipe cards too!

## MATERIALS

- Shadow box frame (6" x 14" [15 x 35–cm] shadow box shown; my spoons measured 12" [30 cm] long)
- Backing material (wood veneer shown; most paper or wood varieties will work well)
- Pen or pencil
- 18" (45-cm) metal ruler with cork back
- Self-healing cutting mat
- X-ACTO knife with #11 blades
- Wooden spoons (3 shown)
- Easy-release tape (such as painter's tape)
- Belt or orbital sander (optional; if needed to flatten the back of the spoons)
- Wood glue

1

1. Remove the backing from the shadow box frame. Lay the backing material over the shadow box frame and trace the outline with a pen or pencil.

**2.** Using the ruler, self-healing cutting mat and X-ACTO knife, line up your ruler and cut out the lines created in step 1 for the backing.

**3.** Arrange the wooden spoons according to your desired spacing and orientation on the backing. Using the ruler, mark the center of each point with a small piece of removable tape. (Tip: If your spoons aren't relatively flat—you will want a ½- to 1-inch [13-mm to 2.5-cm] flat surface for the glue to bond—use a belt sander or orbital sander to flatten a section of the spoons' backs to provide a surface that can adhere evenly to the backing.)

**4.** Apply an even coat of wood glue along the back of each spoon on all parts that will touch the backing.

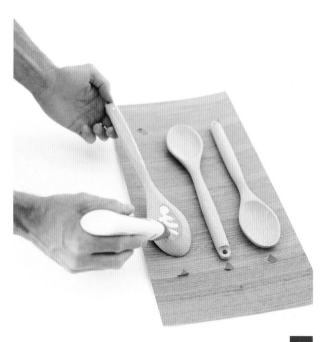

**5.** Line up the spoons on the marks created in step 3. Hold them firmly in place until the glue starts to hold. If needed, place a few heavy books on top to hold the spoons in place while the glue dries. Remove the painter's tape used to mark the spoons' placement.

**6.** Once the glue has fully cured, insert the backing into the shadow box frame.

# GEOMETRIC WOOD VENEER BOX

Time frame: 2 to 4 hours | Workspace: Small

Cabinets are often forgotten for aesthetic touches, but I've found that if something is beautiful and functional, I'm more likely to keep it organized. I'll show you how to make your cabinets both organized and interesting by adding texture and warmth to existing boxes. Utilizing a geometric wood front, you won't believe how quick and simple it is!

## MATERIALS

- Wood veneer with peel-and-stick backing (enough to cover the face of each box; oak shown)
- Wood box (size and quantity dependent on your cabinet)
- Pencil
- Self-healing cutting mat
- X-ACTO knife with #11 blades
- Metal ruler with cork back

1. Start on a square edge of the veneer. Be mindful of the wood grain's direction. For example, I positioned my veneer so one section was straight and another section was diagonal. Each box will use two triangles with two different wood grain directions. For my 4 boxes, I cut 4 pieces of veneer (alternating the direction of wood grain for each piece). Trace the face of the box on a piece of veneer with a pencil. Repeat this process for each box front.

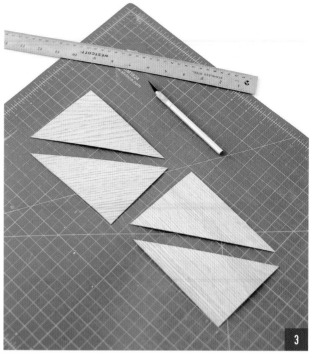

**2.** On a self-healing cutting mat and using the X-ACTO knife and ruler, cut the veneer around the edge of the box front.

**3.** Next, line up the metal ruler on diagonal corners and cut through the wood veneer with the X-ACTO knife.

**4.** Take the back adhesive corner off one of the triangle pieces (I used a vertical grain first). Line the corner up on the box front and press down. Remove the rest of the backing and press the veneer down as you go.

**5.** Select a contrasting veneer piece (I used a diagonal grain). Repeat step 4, but line up the diagonal edge first. Tightly align the wood seam and remove the backing, pressing it down smoothly as you go.

**6.** If you have any pieces that overlap the edge, put the box veneer side down and carefully trim the excess veneer. Without the metal ruler there, it will be easy to trim the box—go slowly and hold the knife straight.

## PROJECT NOTE

The leather tags shown in the image were created from cut leather, a leather stamping kit and brass screw posts.

# ELEVATED HERB PLANTER

Time frame: 2 to 4 hours | Workspace: Small

No room for a large outdoor garden? Create a countertop herb garden to have fresh herbs year-round! One of my favorite parts about meal planning is incorporating fresh herbs from my garden. I love having easy access to them directly from my countertop. Basic materials and an open frame design make the pots easy to remove for watering or maintenance.

## MATERIALS

- ¾" x ½" (19 x 13–mm) oak trim (see Cut List)
- Chop saw (optional)
- Drill and ⅛" (3-mm) countersink bit
- Scrap wood block
- Wood glue
- 8 (1¼" [3-cm]) brass screws
- Stain or sealant of choice (clear wax shown)
- Gloves and rag
- 3 (4" [10-cm]) terra-cotta pots

## CUT LIST

- Top rails: 2 (14" [35-cm]) pieces
- Legs: 4 (3½" [8.75-cm]) pieces
- Bottom rails: 2 (4" [10-cm]) pieces

1

1. Cut the oak trim per the Cut List with a chop saw or have it cut at your local home improvement store. Using a ⅛-inch (3-mm) countersink bit, drill the top rails on the ½-inch (13-mm) side, ⅜ inch (9.5 mm) from each end to create two predrilled holes per top rail. Use a scrap wood block on the back side to protect the surface below. Again, using the countersink bit, drill one hole in each of the legs on the ¾-inch (19-mm) side, ¼ inch (6 mm) from the end to create one predrilled hole per leg).

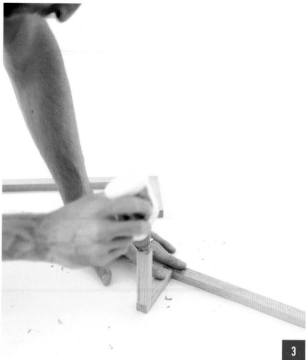

2

3

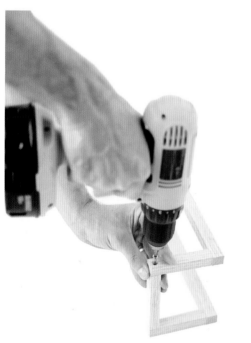

4

**2.** Apply wood glue and screw the top rails to the legs using the brass screws, with the predrilled holes on the legs facing away from the top rails. Ensure the countersink recess on the legs is facing the same direction.

**3.** Apply wood glue on the ends before securing them.

**4.** Screw the legs to the bottom rails.

5

**5.** Once the base is constructed, apply the stain or sealant of your choice to protect the wood (be sure to wear gloves and use a rag).

**6.** Once the stain or sealant is dry, insert the terra-cotta pots. The lips of the pots will rest on the top rails, suspending the pots in the base.

6

# DINING

Small-space living is all about making your space multifunctional, and this is especially true for dining. A table and chairs can easily function both as a dining area and a workspace. In our last apartment, we used a dining table for both eating and a changing station for our son—wiping down before meals, of course! Or, if your dining space is close to your living space, mount a TV above a dining sideboard—you can hang an art canvas over the TV when it's not in use to make it decorative.

Read on to see projects focusing on smart storage that is functional, interesting and streamlined. A trivet that is like a piece of art (no need to put it away), elevated everyday items and high-impact art pieces—so easy and fun to make!

## GET ORGANIZED

- Utilize the center of your table as storage. If you have a collection of dishes (i.e., white jars), store them on the dining table as a centerpiece. Bonus points if you can layer wood cutting boards or a trivet underneath.

- If you own your home, try making recessed wall niches as a modern china cabinet to display dishes.

- Organize your art by vertically running it floor to ceiling (leaving about 6 inches [15 cm] from both floor and ceiling). Add a picture light above to draw attention to the space.

# WOOD SLAT CONSOLE TABLE

Time frame: 2 days | Workspace: Large

We've lived in seven rentals over the past ten years and one of our most-used pieces is a console table. Place baskets underneath for extra storage or ottomans for extra seating. It's perfect as a TV stand, entry table, sofa table, narrow work station and more.

This slat table utilizes simple wood cuts repetitively to create a solid yet airy piece that will blend easily with several different styles. Since this project requires several cuts, we recommend that you cut the wood yourself with a chop saw; if you don't have one, you can rent one at your local home improvement store or you can hire a local carpenter.

## MATERIALS

- 1 x 2 and 1 x 3 oak boards (or similar wood; see Cut List)
- Chop saw (optional)
- 220-grit sanding block or orbital sander (recommended)
- Yardstick
- Pencil
- Wood glue
- Drill with ⅛" (3-mm) countersink bit
- Masking or painter's tape
- 90 (1¼" [3-cm]) wood screws
- 2 wood clamps
- 2 (4" [10-cm]) spring clamps
- Microfiber cloth
- Sealant of choice (optional)

## CUT LIST

- Top: 1 x 2 oak board, cut into 10 (5' [1.5-m]) pieces
- Top spacers: 1 x 2 oak board, cut into 9 (2½" [6.25-cm]) pieces
- Side: 1 x 3 oak board, cut into 20 (28½" [71.25-cm]) pieces
- Side spacers: 1 x 3 oak board, cut into 36 (3" [7.5-cm]) pieces

1. Prepare the 1 x 2 and 1 x 3 oak boards by cutting them with a chop saw or having them cut at your local home improvement store (see the Cut List).

2. Lightly sand the edges of all the pieces with a 220-grit sanding block or orbital sander to remove any rough edges.

3. Using the yardstick and pencil, measure and mark the center of the first top piece, which will be 28¾ inches (72 cm) from the edge. Repeat this process for each 5-foot (1.5-m) top piece. This will be the edge of the center spacer.

**4.** Start building the table by laying 1 (1 x 2) top piece with 2 (1 x 3) side pieces on a flat surface (the 1 x 2 will be on top). Lay out several of the 1 x 3 side spacers: 1 on the bottom left, 1 on the top left, 1 in the middle, 1 on the top right and 1 on the bottom right (i.e., with the 1 x 2 on top and the 1 x 3 on the sides, as noted in the Cut List). Apply wood glue on the back of a side spacer.

**5.** Using a drill fitted with a ⅛-inch (3-mm) countersink bit, predrill two diagonal holes in the bottom-left spacer. Repeat this process for all the remaining spacers: top left, middle, top right and bottom right (i.e., with the 1 x 2 on top and the 1 x 3 on the sides, as noted in the Cut List). The screws will be covered so there is no need to measure. To accommodate the next layer of top and side pieces, the screws will need to alternate from the left side to the right side at each location so as to avoid the screws hitting. (Tip: This step is easiest with two people, one person to install screws and one person to lay out the next boards and place small pieces of tape where the screws should be.)

6

7

8

**6.** Secure the spacer with 2 (1¼-inch [3-cm]) wood screws. Install a side spacer aligned with the bottom edge of the side following the same process from steps 5 and 6. Repeat those steps to install the opposite side and top and bottom side spacers.

**7.** Begin layering the table. Align another 1 x 3 side piece on top of the installed side spacers.

**8.** Use a wood clamp to help hold the side piece in place and predrill one hole into the top and bottom into the side spacers below. Remove the side piece, apply wood glue to the spacers, reinstall the side piece and secure it with screws. Repeat steps 4 through 7, installing new sections until one row (the top and two sides) remains.

9. On the last row, apply wood glue to each of the spacer pieces. Align and set the sides and top pieces in place.

10. Use 4-inch (10-cm) spring clamps to secure the final glued row to the previous row until the glue has cured.

11. Using a 220-grit sanding block or orbital sander, lightly sand all of the joined edges to remove any excess wood glue. (Note: If possible, sand outside—since this is a larger surface, it will produce more dust.)

**12.** Wipe the entire table with a microfiber cloth to remove any dust.

**13.** Apply the sealant of your choice (if desired) to protect the finished table.

# LONG WOODEN TRIVET

Time frame: 2 to 4 hours | Workspace: Small

I don't know about you, but one of the things I dislike about setting the table is placing several trivets randomly around the table for hot dishes. It looks messy and unintentional. We've solved that problem by creating a long trivet that can hold multiple dishes. The construction is simple, but it's durable and made to last. A bonus is that it also looks great, so it can stay on the table when not in use! This trivet is perfect for small-space living—it doesn't need to take up valuable cabinet space.

## MATERIALS

- 10 (3' [90-cm]) 1 x 2 oak board pieces (or similar wood)
- Chop saw (optional)
- Yardstick
- Pencil
- Drill with 1" (2.5-cm) Forstner bit
- Scrap wood to protect surface when drilling
- Wood clamp
- 3 (14¼" [36.25-cm]) 1" (2.5-cm) diameter dowel rod pieces (walnut shown)
- Hammer
- 30 (1" [2.5-cm]) finishing nails
- Sealant of choice

1

1. Cut the 1 x 2 oak pieces or have them cut at your local home improvement store. Ensure that the scale will accommodate place settings at the sides and both ends of your table. The 3-foot (90-cm) trivet was scaled for a 90 x 40–inch (2.25 x 1–m) table. With a yardstick, measure 1 inch (2.5 cm) from the end of a 3-foot (90-cm) board and make a mark with a pencil. Measure the width and make another mark, creating an X to find the center of the hole to be drilled. Repeat this process for the other end and center of the 3-foot (90-cm) board.

2

3

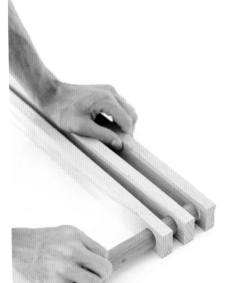

4

**2.** With the drill fitted with the 1-inch (2.5-cm) Forstner bit and a piece of scrap wood below the 3-foot (90-cm) board, drill a hole through the wood on all marks made in step 1. You should have 1-inch (2.5-cm) holes on both ends and in the center of the first 3-foot (90-cm) piece of oak.

**3.** Continue to drill through the rest of the 3-foot (90-cm) pieces of wood. To ensure that the holes line up, align the board with the holes drilled in step 2 with a piece of undrilled wood and clamp them together with a wood clamp. Place a piece of scrap wood below the clamped pieces and drill through them with the 1-inch (2.5-cm) Forstner bit.

**4.** Once three holes are drilled in each piece of wood, insert a wood dowel in the ends and the center.

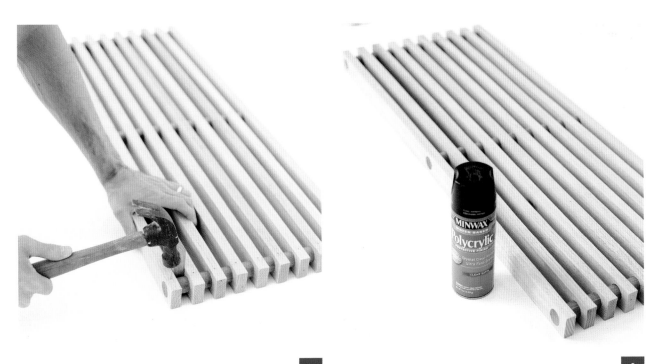

**5.** Space the pieces of wood with a scrap piece of 1 x 2 board and secure the dowels in place by hammering a finishing nail through the scrap piece of 1 x 2 board into the dowel at each intersection.

**6.** Once all the nails are inserted, seal the wood with the sealant of your choice. Be sure to apply the sealant and allow it to dry in a well-ventilated space (outdoors is best).

# DIP-DYED NAPKINS

Time frame: 2 to 4 hours | Workspace: Small

I love to add cloth napkins to elevate table settings. Whether it's Thanksgiving or a gathering with friends, the extra layer adds so much!

Dip-dying gives an organic feel (i.e., you can't mess it up) that is easy to achieve. Pair your napkins with wooden napkin rings or simply fold them and layer silverware on top for a fuss-free table setting.

## MATERIALS

- Natural-fiber cloth napkins (20" x 20" [50 x 50–cm] white cotton napkin shown)
- Plastic sheet
- Disposable gloves
- Container for dye (dye may transfer)
- Water (as needed)
- Dye of choice (Rit All-Purpose Dye shown in Kelly Green and Wine)
- Stir stick (dye may transfer)
- Paper towel

1. Prewash and dry the napkins, and protect your work surface with a plastic sheet.

2. Put on the disposable gloves. Prepare the dye bath by filling up a container with about 5 inches (12.5 cm) of warm water. Add the dye of your choice. If the dye color is too intense out of the bottle, add a little of the complementary color. For example, I added a little Wine dye to the dye bath.

**3.** Stir the dye mixture with the stir stick.

**4.** Test the color of the dye bath by dipping a paper towel in the dye bath. Adjust the color as needed.

**5.** Hold the napkin by one corner and dip the napkin in the dye bath for just a few seconds. Pull the napkin up a few inches to allow the dye to saturate for a few minutes. Repeat this process, continuing to pull the napkin up gradually and allowing the dye to soak in. If it is easier, allow the napkin to rest on the side of the container. The goal is to leave a gradient from light to dark.

**6.** Once the desired color is achieved, remove the napkin from the dye bath and squeeze the excess dye out with the lighter side at the top. Place the napkin flat on the plastic sheet to dry. Repeat steps 5 and 6 with the remaining napkins.

**7.** Wash the napkins per the instructions on the dye bottle before using.

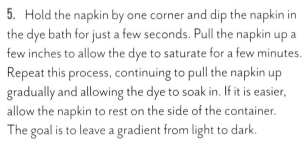

# DYED RIPPED PAPER ABSTRACT ART

Time frame: 1 day | Workspace: Small

This project evolved in the midst of creating projects for the book, and I love the outcome! Math isn't my strong suit (David and I balance each other well), so I love creating something that requires zero measuring and still looks amazing.

This dyed and ripped paper art is exactly that—you don't need any art experience to have a great outcome! I love the rich, saturated colors (though that part is completely up to you).

## MATERIALS

- 2 watercolor sheets (22" x 30" [55 x 75–cm] sheet shown)
- Metal yardstick
- Disposable gloves
- Plastic sheet
- Water (as needed)
- Bucket for dye bath (dye may transfer)
- Dye and watercolor paint of choice
- Paper towel
- Watercolor brush
- Cup for water (dye may transfer)
- Scissors
- Modge Podge®
- 1" (2.5-cm) foam brush
- Frame of choice (24" x 35¾" [60 x 90–cm] frame shown)

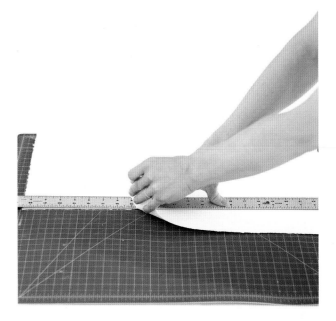

1

1. On a flat surface, place the short side of the paper (e.g., the 22-inch [55-cm] side is shown) and place the yardstick on top parallel to the edge of the paper and 1 to 2 inches (2.5 to 5 cm) from the edge. Hold the ruler with your nondominant hand and tear a strip with your dominant hand to give a ripped edge. Continue this process, creating strips of paper. The pieces of paper should be a variety of widths ranging from ½ inch (13 mm) to about 5 inches (12.5 cm) wide.

2. Put on disposable gloves and lay out the plastic sheet to protect the work surface. Add 4 to 6 inches (10 to 15 cm) of water to the bucket. In the bucket, add the dye to prepare your dye bath to reach the color of your choice. Test the dye bath color with a white paper towel and adjust as needed. (Note: The color mixes shown are Rit All-Purpose Dye in Navy Blue with a small amount of Lemon Yellow added to make it less purple and more neutral; and equal parts Rit All-Purpose Dye in Tangerine and Rit All-Purpose Dye in Wine with a small amount of Rit All-Purpose Dye in Kelly Green to make it less intense). Add strips of paper to the dye bath. Allow the paper to soften as the water absorbs and fold it to fit in your container. Allow some strips of paper to sit longer to achieve different color values. Also, allow some strips of paper to sit on the dye bath's surface so the dye absorbs differently, creating a variated surface.

3. Once the desired color value is reached, remove the paper strips from the dye bath and lay them on the plastic sheet to dry.

**4.** Next, create a few strips of paper by painting watercolor directly on the paper with a watercolor brush. Using the cup, apply a light wash of water over the entire surface and add darker areas as desired.

**5.** Once all the strips of paper are dry, begin laying them out on the other watercolor sheet. Lay some strips at a slight angle, some the partial width and some the full width. Disperse the color evenly.

**6.** Trim any excess edges with scissors.

7

8

9

**7.** Take extra pieces and disperse them throughout, layering under the other strips, varying the width of the strips shown.

**8.** Once your desired composition is achieved, adhere the strips to the base sheet of paper. Apply Modge Podge to the backs of the strips with a foam brush. (Note: I found it easiest to work in sections, connecting any strips that intersected first and then adhering them to the paper below.)

**9.** Once all the strips are attached, trim any excess strips at the edge.

**10.** Mount the art in the frame of your choice.

# SHIBORI-DYED TABLECLOTH

Time frame: 2 to 4 hours | Workspace: Medium

I've been dying items with *shibori*-inspired methods—ways of embellishing textiles by folding and binding fabric and submersing them in a dye bath—for a few years now, and it's addicting! The technique is highly flexible and looks great in several applications. I'd never tried a larger surface, so I wanted to give that a go. This dying technique is all about the folds and a tight binding (which is especially important for larger surfaces).

## MATERIALS

- Natural-fiber tablecloth (57" x 98" [142.5 x 245–cm] white cotton tablecloth shown)
- Iron
- Drop cloth
- Ruler
- Chop saw (optional)
- 2 binding blocks (7" x 7" [18 x 18–cm], ½" [13-mm] thick plywood shown)
- 2 (6" [15-cm]) wood clamps
- 6 (22" [55-cm]) zip ties
- Plastic sheet
- Disposable gloves
- Water (as needed)
- Bucket for dye bath (dye may transfer)
- Dye of choice (Rit All-Purpose Dye in Navy Blue, Black and Lemon Yellow shown)
- Paper towel
- Scissors
- Rit ColorStay Dye Fixative (optional)

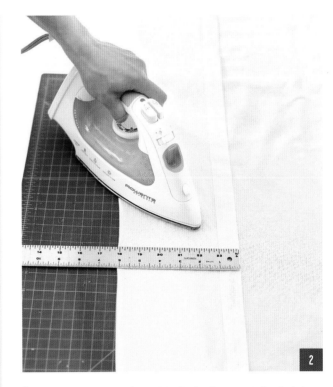

1. Prewash and dry the tablecloth. Once it is dry, lightly iron it if needed. It doesn't need to be perfect, but shouldn't have any large wrinkles.

2. Place the drop cloth on the work surface to protect the surface from heat. Lay the tablecloth on the work surface, with the shorter side toward you. Fold the edge over 6 inches (15 cm), measuring with the ruler, and iron the edge.

**3.** Fold the tablecloth in a zigzag pattern, aligning the fabric as you go, keeping the fold consistently at 6 inches (15 cm). For each fold, iron the edge with the iron.

**4.** Once the entire tablecloth is folded, measuring 6 inches (15 cm) from one end, fold one end up to create a square shape.

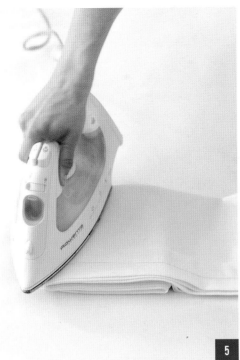

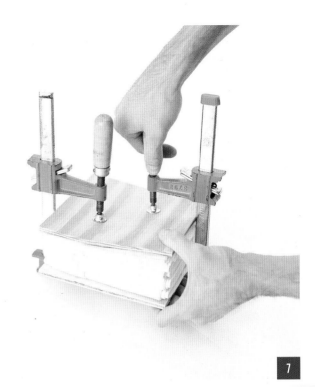

**5.** Alternate the direction of the fold at 6 inches (15 cm), creating a zigzag pattern. Iron to crease as you go.

**6.** Cut the binding blocks yourself or ask your local home improvement store for remnant pieces. Most any wood larger than the folded tablecloth will work.

**7.** To create a grid and prevent the dye from soaking through the entire piece, the binding blocks will need to be tied tightly. Place the wood clamps so they are close to the center of the wood, gradually tightening the clamps to compress the fabric.

**8.** Place the zip ties around all sides and down the middle. Pull until the ties are very tight.

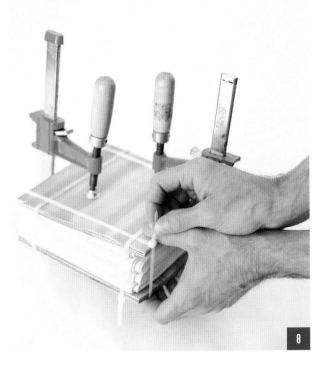

**9.** Once the zip ties are secure and tight, remove the wood clamps.

**10.** Place the plastic sheet on the work surface and put on disposable gloves. Prepare the dye bath. Place warm water, enough to cover the bound tablecloth, in the bucket. Add the dye of your choice. (Note: Rit Navy Blue with a little Rit Black and Lemon Yellow, to neutralize the purple tone of the navy, shown.)

**11.** Test the dye bath color with a small piece of paper towel and adjust the color as needed.

**12.** Fully submerge the bound tablecloth in the dye bath for just a few seconds and remove it. Examine the edges and peel back the folds a little to make sure that the dye has reached all the edges.

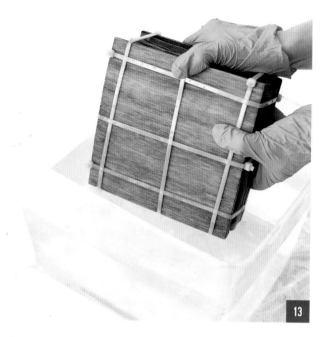

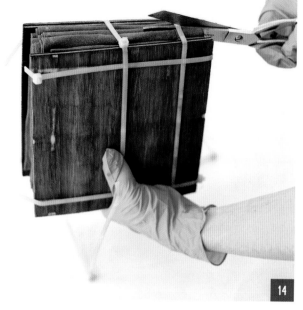

**13.** Once the desired color is reached, with the zip ties still attached, rinse the edges with cool, clean water, either in a bucket or under running water (a utility sink is recommended, as the dye may transfer).

**14.** Once the water runs fairly clean, remove the zip ties with scissors.

**15.** With the tablecloth still folded, rinse the edges again, squeezing as you go, until the water runs completely clear.

**16.** Unfold the tablecloth and rinse, then wash per the dye manufacturer's directions. For added color-transfer protection, Rit ColorStay Dye Fixative can be added (follow the manufacturer's instructions).

# BEDROOM

Small-space living almost always means a smaller bedroom, but that doesn't mean you need to sacrifice function or aesthetics. Using smart, space-saving solutions will allow for everything you need and make your bedroom a space you love spending time in.

This chapter focuses on using ready-made objects in new ways or adding a twist to customize them.

## GET ORGANIZED

- Tired of looking at that lamp or charger cord under your nightstand? Hide cords by attaching small Command™ Products strips down the leg of your nightstand and placing cords in the clips.

- If you have a drawer in your nightstand, drill a hole in the back panel and run cords into the drawer to charge your phone in your nightstand.

- No nightstand? Stack a few vintage suitcases to maximize storage (this is a perfect solution for storing items you don't use every day) and have a place to rest your drink at night.

# TABLE RUNNER TO LONG LUMBAR PILLOW

Time frame: 1 hour | Workspace: Small

Long lumbar pillows are popular now, and for good reason. They make a big statement on the bed. Plus, making the bed is easy—lots of impact in a long pillow—perfect for layering in front of smaller ones!

Utilizing a premade table runner, this project requires zero sewing but has the look of a custom pillow. It's fast, too, taking only about an hour to complete.

## MATERIALS

- Lumbar pillow (50" x 14" [125 x 35–cm] memory foam body pillow shown; this size will work for a queen or king bed)
- Tape measure
- Table runner, presewn with layers of fabric (72" x 14" [180 x 35–cm] table runner shown)
- Pencil
- Scissors
- Seam ripper or X-ACTO knife with #11 blades
- Permanent fabric glue

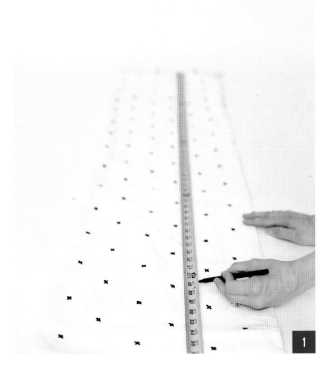

1. Measure the lumbar pillow with a tape measure to confirm the measurements. Lay the table runner out. Starting on the bottom seam, measure the length of the lumbar pillow and add 3 inches (7.5 cm). Make a mark with the pencil, repeat the process and make another mark. Connect the dots and draw a line with the pencil.

2. Cut the table runner with scissors along the line created in step 1.

3. On the end cutoff in step 2 (the smaller end, which you will not be using), if applicable, carefully remove the fringe with a seam ripper or X-ACTO knife.

4. Insert the lumbar pillow into the open end of the table runner. (Note: I found it works best to bunch several inches of fabric up and then pull it forward.)

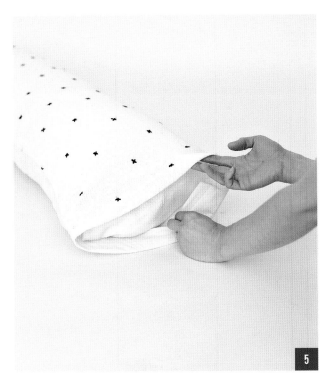

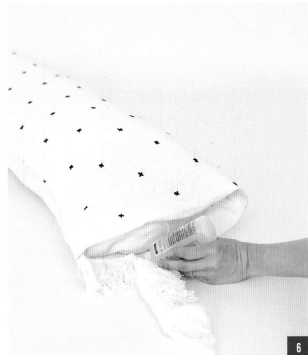

**5.** Once the lumbar pillow is completely in the table runner, fold the edge inside. Pinch the 2 edges together to test how close it is to the lumbar pillow. Adjust as needed and confirm that all edges meet and are even with the edge of the pillow.

**6.** Apply a line of permanent fabric glue on the bottom edge of the pillow opening and apply the fringe removed in step 3 as you go. Typically, the glue dries quickly, so only apply a few inches and press the fringe in place.

**7.** Once the fringe is connected at the bottom, apply permanent fabric glue to the top of the fringe and close the pillow sham as you go, ensuring that the top edge is even.

# LEATHER-WRAPPED SHADE SCONCE

Time frame: 2 to 4 hours | Workspace: Small

Sconces are the perfect space-saving lighting solution—they don't take up valuable space on top of nightstands. Also, they are often low-profile, so they don't protrude far, working well with narrower nightstands.

After drooling over custom leather sconces that have been popping up in my feed over the years, I decided to create my own version. Modifying an existing sconce makes it super easy!

## MATERIALS

- Existing sconce (a cone, fabric or metal shade; LED bulb recommended; Meta from the Mitzi collection by Hudson Valley Lighting shown)
- Tools to remove hardware from the sconce (if needed; offset Phillips head screwdriver to remove hardware on the sconce)
- Paper for template (such as one large piece of paper that will wrap around the entire shade with overhang on all sides or a few pieces of printer paper taped together)
- Painter's tape
- Pen or pencil
- Measuring tape
- Scissors
- 1 yard (90-cm) leather (such as from the Leather Hide Store), quantity dependent on the shade's size
- Self-healing cutting mat
- X-ACTO knife with #11 blades
- Permanent glue (such as Aleene's Fast Grab Tacky Glue)

1. If applicable, remove any hardware from the sconce shade with tools. Leave the wiring intact.

2. Prepare the template by wrapping 1 large piece of paper (or a few pieces of paper taped together) completely around the shade with overlap on all sides. Use painter's tape to keep the paper in place. If applicable, work around the lamp wiring by carefully trimming the paper to fit.

3. Trace around the top and bottom of the shade (and the sides as well, if needed) with a pen or pencil. Be careful not to mark the shade. Using the measuring tape, measure out about ½ inch (13 mm) on the top and bottom (this extra leather will be trimmed off later).

4. Remove the template from the sconce shade and cut out along the line with scissors.

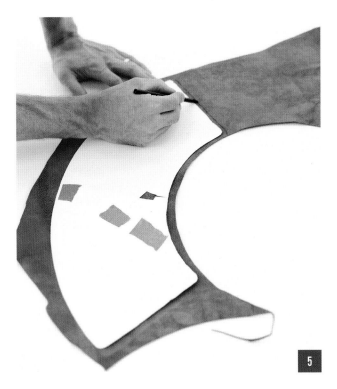

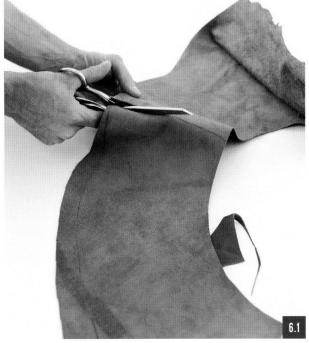

**5.** Place the template on the back side of the leather and trace it with a pen or pencil.

**6.** Using scissors, follow the line created in step 5 and cut out the overall shape. On the self-healing cutting mat, use the X-ACTO knife to cut out the space for the electrical wires.

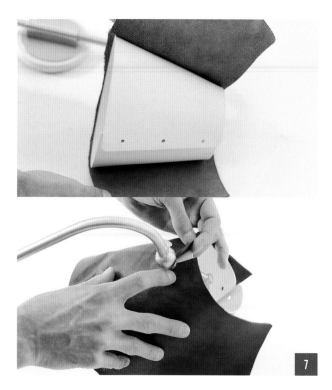

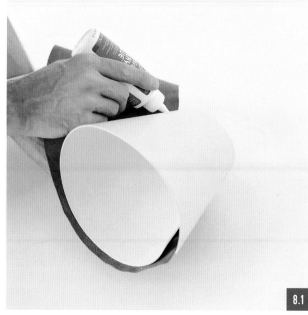

7. Line up the leather on the shade so there is extra on the top and bottom and, starting at one end, begin securing it to the shade with the permanent glue.

8. As you go, smooth the leather so there are no bubbles and secure it at the end with more glue.

9. Once the glue has dried, trim off the excess leather carefully with sharp scissors along the edge of the shade.

10. If your shade has hardware, carefully trim holes with an X-ACTO knife and reinstall the hardware.

# TASSEL END-OF-BED THROW FROM TABLECLOTH

Time frame: 2 to 4 hours | Workspace: Medium

I love gorgeous end-of-bed throws with tassels! Large throws work especially well for smaller spaces because they don't take up valuable closet space and can be used when you have guests in town or as a throw for the sofa. I recently splurged on one (my general rule for bigger items is to buy if I can't keep them out of my mind for more than a year). But I also love a deal and a good DIY, so after reader requests, I've created a DIY version for a lot less.

If you've had your eye on an oversized throw, but you're not ready to take the plunge, try DIYing first!

## MATERIALS

- Cardboard tassel template (2½" x 4" [6.25 x 10–cm] shown)
- Scissors
- Yarn of choice
- Natural-fiber tablecloth, prewashed and dried (60" x 84" [150 x 210–cm] cotton seersucker tablecloth shown; will fit the end of a queen bed)
- Yardstick
- Painter's tape
- Large needle (such as a #16 needle)

1

**1.** Cut the cardboard template to size with scissors (2½ x 4–inch [6.25 x 10–cm] shown). The height of the template will be the overall length of the tassel.

**2.** To start creating the tassel, hold the end of the yarn on the end of the template with the thumb of your dominant hand.

**3.** Wind the yarn around the template by moving the hand with the template and holding the yarn down. Once the string holds, remove your thumb. Keep the yarn as straight as possible (this will help keep the tassel neat). Continue to wind the yarn around until the desired thickness is achieved. To test this, pinch the front and back of the yarn. This will give you a general idea of the thickness to expect with each tassel. Don't worry, it doesn't need to be exact to look great!

**4.** Repeat step 3 to create the desired number of tassels. For example, for my 60 x 84–inch (150 x 210–cm) tablecloth (applying tassels to the 60-inch [150-cm] sides), I used 8 tassels per side.

**5.** Cut a piece of yarn about 8 inches (20 cm) long. This will be the top piece that will connect to the tablecloth and will be trimmed later. Slide one end under the top of the bunch of yarn. Pull tightly and tie a double knot.

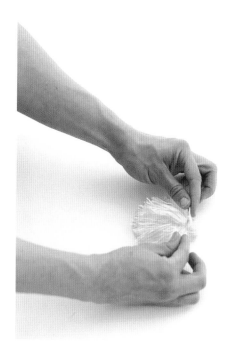

**6.** Pull the yarn off of the cardboard template. Slide a pair of sharp scissors through the end, so the string tied in step 5 is on the opposite side. Pull tightly on the yarn and cut the loops with the scissors.

**7.** Cut a piece of yarn about 8 inches (20 cm) long and secure the tassel. About ½ inch (13 mm) down from the top of the tassel, tie a single knot, flip the tassel over and tie another single knot. The tie will self-tighten. Do this several times until the yarn holds itself. To finish the knot, alternate which yarn is on the top as you tie. This will help prevent the tassel from unraveling.

**8.** If desired, create a second tie, about ¼ inch (6 mm) from the tie created in step 7. Repeat step 7.

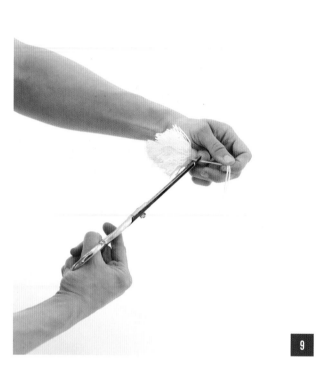

9. Trim off excess yarn from steps 6 and 7 with scissors.

10. Once the tassel is secure, shake it out so the yarn expands. Trim any long pieces of yarn with scissors.

11. Lay your tablecloth out. Facing the short end (the 60-inch [150-cm] end shown), loosely lay the tassels out to determine the desired spacing (9 inches [23 cm] shown). With a yardstick, measure equal spacing, with tassels on both ends. Mark the tassel placements with painter's tape.

**12.** Thread the end of the top of the tassel through the needle and secure the tassels at the points marked in step 11.

**13.** Secure the tassels by tying the ends, alternating what yarn is on top. This will increase the durability of the tassels.

**14.** Once the tassels are secure, trim off excess yarn with scissors. Remove the painter's tape.

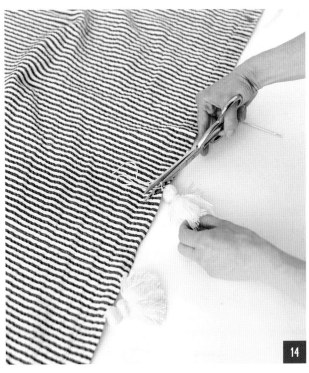

# FLOATING NIGHTSTAND
## with Fabric-Wrapped Drawer and Leather Pull

Time frame: 2 days | Workspace: Medium

This is the new and improved version of a nightstand from one of our first rentals. We've ditched the legs and made it floating—perfect for adding a basket for extra storage underneath or a stool so the nightstand can double as a small vanity. Utilizing an existing drawer and building a box around it, the process is fairly simple and can be completed in a weekend!

We've provided two cutting methods, straight or mitered. If you're getting the wood cut at your local home improvement store, we recommend straight cuts. For more information, see the project note.

## MATERIALS
### DRAWER

- IKEA Skubb box with compartments (17¼" x 13½" x 4¼" [43 x 33.75 x 10.6 cm])
- Drawer front face board (¼" [6-mm] plywood or 30-ply chipboard, cut to 4⅜" x 17⅜" [11 x 43.5 cm] for the IKEA Skubb box with compartments)
- Chop saw (optional)
- Ruler
- Pencil
- Scrap wood block
- Drill with ⅛" (3-mm) and ¼" (6-mm) bits
- ½ yard (45 cm) fabric
- Scissors
- Permanent glue for wood and fabric (Aleene's® Quick Dry Tacky Glue™ shown)
- Foam brush
- #14 upholstery needle
- Upholstery thread (to match fabric)

### LEATHER PULL

- Leather (enough to cut out a 1¼" x 4½" [3 x 11.25–cm] rectangle; leather from Leather Hide Store shown)
- Ruler
- Pencil
- Scissors
- Leather punch (or X-ACTO knife)
- ½" (13-mm) brass binding post

### WOOD BOX

- ¾" (19-mm) birch plywood
- Wood glue
- Clamps (masking or painter's tape can be used)
- 4 (2" [5-cm]) inside-corner angle brackets (to mount to wall)
- 220-grit sanding block
- ¾" (19-mm) birch veneer tape (optional)
- Iron
- Sealant of choice

**Cut List for Mitered Corners**

- ¾" (19-mm) birch plywood
- Top and bottom: 2 (19¹⁄₁₆" [48 cm] wide x 13¾" [34.4 cm] deep) pieces
- Sides: 2 (6" [15 cm] high x 13¾" [34.4 cm] deep) pieces

**Cut List for Straight Edges**

- ¾" (19-mm) birch plywood
- Top and bottom: 2 (19¹⁄₁₆" [48 cm] wide x 13¾" [34.4 cm] deep) pieces
- Sides: 2 (4½" [11.25 cm] high x 13¾" [34.4 cm] deep) pieces

**1.** Start by creating a drawer face for the IKEA Skubb box. Measure the box face and cut the drawer front face board slightly larger. (For example, for the IKEA Skubb box's 17¼ x 4¼–inch [43 x 10.6–cm] drawer face, cut the face board to 17⅜ x 4⅜ inches [43.5 x 11 cm].)

**2.** To measure hole placement (to be used to secure the face board to the drawer front) use a ruler to measure ⅜ inch (9.5 mm) from each edge for the corner hole and mark the spot with a pencil. From that mark, measure ⅜ inch (9.5 mm) along each side and mark ⅜ inch (9.5 mm) from the edge with a pencil.

**3.** Place the face board on a scrap wood block. With a drill fitted with a ⅛-inch (3-mm) bit, drill through each mark created in step 2.

**4.** Place the drawer face on the fabric and use scissors to cut the fabric out around the drawer face, leaving a 1-inch (2.5-cm) border of fabric around the drawer face. If your fabric has a pattern, be mindful of how that looks on the front, keeping the fabric straight. Apply the permanent glue with the foam brush to the front of the face board. Adhere the face board to the back of the fabric.

**5.** Finish the edges by trimming the fabric at the corners, leaving about $1/16$ inch (2 mm) of fabric at the corners. Fold the fabric over, securing it to the back of the face board.

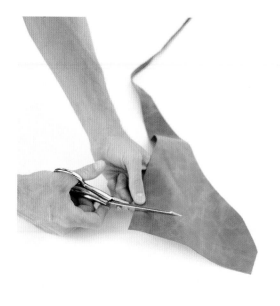

6

7

9

**6.** Create the leather pull for the nightstand. On the back of the piece of leather, measure and trace a 1¼ x 4½ inch (3 x 11.25 cm) rectangle.

**7.** Cut out the rectangle traced in step 6 with scissors.

**8.** Using a ruler and pencil, mark three holes on the leather rectangle. The holes will be centered at ⅜ inch (9.5 mm), 3 inches (7.5 cm) and 4⅛ inches (10.5 cm).

**9.** Cut out the holes with a leather punch. The holes don't need to be perfect. If you don't have a leather punch, use an X-ACTO knife.

10

11

**10.** With a drill fitted with a ¼-inch (6-mm) bit, drill a hole in the center of the drawer face, ⅜ inch (9.5 mm) down from the top.

**11.** Fold the leather over so the bottom and middle holes align and place the brass binding post through the holes. On the back side of the drawer face, fold the leather over and secure the other side of the brass binding post.

**12.** Thread the #14 upholstery needle with upholstery thread to match the fabric. Align the drawer face so it is centered on the front of the IKEA Skubb box. Through the holes created in step 3, secure the face board to the box front on all corners.

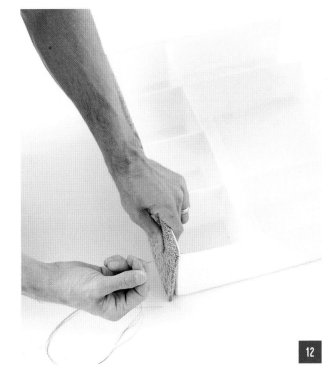

12

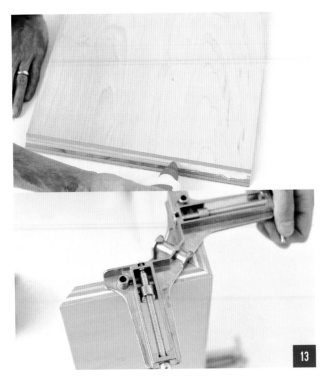

**13.** Begin assembling the wood box which will go around the drawer front. Join the bottom and sides by applying wood glue and using clamps to secure them together (or you can use tape to hold them in place once the glue starts to hold).

**14.** On the top, using the drill, secure the angle brackets 4 inches (10 cm) from each end.

**15.** Finish assembling the box by applying wood glue to the seams and using clamps (or tape) to secure the box while it dries.

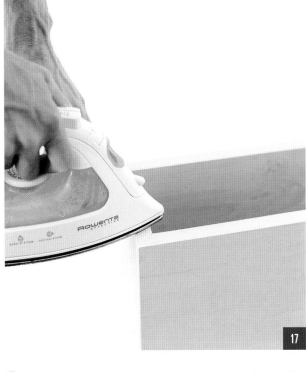

**16.** Sand any rough edges with a 220-grit sanding block.

**17.** If desired, conceal the plywood edge on the front of the box by applying birch veneer with the iron, following the instructions on the package. Apply the wood sealant of choice, such as clear matte polyurethane.

**PROJECT NOTE**

All the measurements in the materials list are for the IKEA Skubb box with compartments (17¼" x 13½" x 4¼" [43 x 33.75 x 10.6 cm]).

# TRIPTYCH PLANT ART

Time frame: 2 to 4 hours | Workspace: Medium

This is a variation on one of the most popular projects on my site and shop! We show you how to make your own tropical leaf print, split into three pieces to form one piece of art. It's perfect for adding organic color and texture to your space. For a bedroom, I love this hung over a bed, but it also works in other spaces, such as above a desk or dining table.

## MATERIALS

- Plant of choice (split-leaf philodendron shown; see project notes)
- White background (such as a tabletop or large sheet of white paper)
- Objects of various heights or thread
- Camera of choice
- Photo editing software of choice (see project notes)
- Printer of choice, to create 3 (16" x 24" [40 x 60–cm]) prints (art shown printed and framed through Mpix)

1. Next to a window with directional light, place the plant on its side on a large white background. Adjust the leaves' direction and placement. If needed, place objects under the leaves to raise them (or tie thread onto the stems to pull the leaves in different directions). If needed for composition, trim a few leaves off and place them on the paper.

2

**2.** Once the desired leaf placement is achieved, photograph the leaves with the camera. (Note: For a triptych, an elongated landscape photo, such as one created using panoramic mode, is preferred to avoid cropping the image).

**3.** Adjust the lighting and color of the photo in the photo editing software of your choice.

**4.** Crop the photo into three equally sized images using the photo editing software.

**5.** Print and frame the photos at a local print shop or an online printer (such as Mpix).

### PROJECT NOTES

• Large leaves work well to produce a variety of values as the light hits the leaf. Split-leaf philodendron can be found at your local nursery or home improvement store.

• You can use a program like Adobe Photoshop. The Photoshop Express app for mobile phones is a free option.

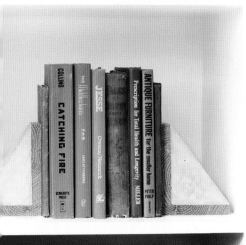

# WORKSPACE

Sometimes you don't need an entire room for a workspace. Whether it's carving out a corner of your living room or utilizing a wide entry, it's possible to create your own workspace. Recently, we turned a small space off of our bedroom into an office for David. We added a custom built-in from floor to ceiling and around the door, a few furniture pieces and DIY projects to work as an office. It was a functionless space that collected odds and ends, but now it's a space that works as David's home office. Review your floorplan and see if there's a small space that could work for you: You can use a corner or a space under the stairs or you can even convert a closet into a workspace by removing the doors and adding a built-in desk (bonus for adding shelving above).

In this chapter, we'll show you how to make simple, impactful art—and you might already have all the materials on hand! We'll also demonstrate creative storage solutions that are both practical and beautiful, keeping everyday items within reach but concealed.

## GET ORGANIZED

- Empty wall? Add a large pegboard (or place several together to give the appearance of one large board) across the entire span. It can function as an art piece while providing versatile, flexible storage that can be changed as needed.

- Add shelving to your space. Looking for something simple? Purchase a few wall brackets and add a wood top. You can purchase different lengths at your local home improvement store. They are typically available up to 12 feet (3.6 m). For most applications, you will need a bracket about every 3 feet (90 cm). Be sure to locate the wall studs to mount the bracket.

- Printer inside a cabinet? Add a slide-out shelf so it's easy to access!

# DYED TAPE GEOMETRIC ART

Time frame: 1 day | Workspace: Small

I love art that is simple, impactful and easy to make. This ribbon art is a favorite because it is completely customizable to match your décor. Utilizing white cotton twill tape, you are in control of the color by mixing your own dye. You're also in control of the size; whether you have a small or large wall, you can easily adjust the measurements to fit your space.

With minimal materials, this project can easily be created with just a few hours of working time.

## MATERIALS

- Paper of choice, cut to size if needed (white mixed media paper works well; 16" x 20" [40 x 50–cm] sheet shown)
- Pencil
- Ruler
- Scissors or X-ACTO knife with #11 blades
- Gridded self-healing cutting mat
- Hot water
- 1 plastic container for each dye color (dye may transfer)
- Dye of choice (mix of Rit All-Purpose Dye in Navy Blue, Tangerine, Lemon Yellow, Wine and Kelly Green shown)
- Paper towels
- 6 yards (5.4 m) 1" (2.5-cm) white cotton twill tape (or other natural-fiber fabric or ribbon)
- Disposable gloves and plastic sheet
- Glue for fabric and paper (such as Modge Podge)
- 16" x 20" (40 x 50–cm) frame

1. Prepare a piece of paper to fit in the frame by removing the paper insert or backing from the frame and tracing on your paper with a pencil. Cut it out with a metal ruler and scissors or an X-ACTO knife on a self-healing cutting mat.

**2.** Prepare the dye baths. Add a few inches of hot water to each plastic container. Add the main color desired for the dye bath and add secondary colors in small amounts. (Tip: Test the dye bath with a white paper towel as you go. If the colors are too intense, add a small amount of the complementary colors to make them less saturated. Mixes shown are equal parts Rit All-Purpose Dye in Wine and Tangerine with a splash of Kelly Green; Navy Blue with a splash of Lemon Yellow; and Kelly Green with a splash of Wine.)

**3.** Cut the twill tape into smaller pieces to dye. Determine the approximate size needed. For example, for my 16 x 20–inch (40 x 50–cm) frame, I cut 36 x 3–inch (90 x 7.5–cm) and 18 x 6–inch (45 x 15–cm) pieces. These pieces will later be cut to size.

**4.** Put on disposable gloves and lay out the plastic sheet. On the plastic sheet, dye the twill tape by dipping it in the dye bath. Once the desired color is achieved, remove the twill tape from the dye bath and allow it to dry on the plastic sheet.

**5.** Determine the desired twill tape length and pattern. (Note: Grid paper or a computer program such as AutoCAD or Adobe Illustrator work well for this.) For example, for my 16 x 20–inch (40 x 50–cm) frame, my twill tape pieces from inside to outside measured 8 inches (20 cm; left side), 3 inches (7.5 cm; top), 10 inches (25 cm; right side), 5 inches (12.5 cm; bottom), 12 inches (30 cm; left side), 7 inches (18 cm; top), 14 inches (35 cm; right side), 9 inches (23 cm; bottom), 16 inches (40 cm; left side), 11 inches (28 cm; top) and 16 inches (40 cm; end, right side). Each transition increases by 2 inches (5 cm) to account for the 1-inch (2.5-cm) twill tape and 1-inch (2.5-cm) spacing. The end piece is the same dimension as the last parallel piece.

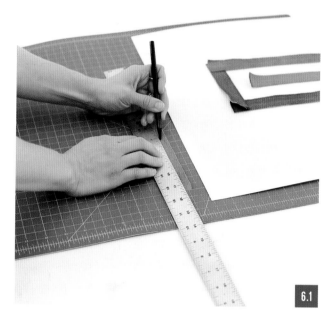

**6.1**

**6.2**

**6.** Start laying the twill tape out on the paper. It doesn't need to be perfect (you will measure later). Decide how you want to distribute the colors. Next, cut the twill tape to size. Measure and mark the length on the twill tape and cut it with scissors. Roughly lay it out as you go.

**7.** Once all the pieces are cut to length, cut a 45-degree angle where applicable. Referring to the layout created in step 6, determine the direction of the 45-degree angle. Each piece will have two (45-degree) angles—with the exception of the first and last, which will have only one (45-degree) angle—like a picture frame. Create all the cuts and lay them out as you go. On the cutting mat, line the corner of the twill tape with the 45-degree line on the cutting mat, align the ruler over the twill tape on the 45-degree line and mark it with a pencil. Cut the pencil mark with scissors. (Note: Carefully align the twill tape and ruler each time, as this will ensure even corners where the pieces meet.)

**7**

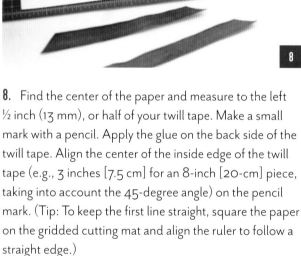

**8.** Find the center of the paper and measure to the left ½ inch (13 mm), or half of your twill tape. Make a small mark with a pencil. Apply the glue on the back side of the twill tape. Align the center of the inside edge of the twill tape (e.g., 3 inches [7.5 cm] for an 8-inch [20-cm] piece, taking into account the 45-degree angle) on the pencil mark. (Tip: To keep the first line straight, square the paper on the gridded cutting mat and align the ruler to follow a straight edge.)

**9.** Continue to work around the piece, lining up the corners of the pieces. Either reference the previous piece of twill tape or the ruler to keep a straight line. It doesn't need to be perfect, but this will keep the layout fairly straight. Apply the glue as you go until you reach the last piece. Once the glue is dry, transfer the art to the frame.

# GLASS CYLINDER TO PENCIL DISPENSER

Time frame: 2 to 4 hours | Workspace: Small

Inspired by straw dispensers and French presses, this pencil dispenser is functional and beautiful at the same time—perfect for small-space living! A few nontraditional materials, such as a candle hurricane and threaded rods, become a beautiful way to display pencils.

## MATERIALS

- 2 (3½" [8.75-cm] diameter, ½" [13-mm] thick) wood disks (white oak shown; see project notes)
- 1 (4" [10-cm], ½" [13-mm] thick) wood disk (white oak shown; see project notes)
- 220-grit sandpaper
- Microfiber cloth
- Wood glue
- Ruler
- Pencil
- Scrap wood block
- Drill with ¼" (6-mm) and ⅜" (9.5-mm) bits
- 2 (¼" [6–mm], 20-thread count) brass connector caps
- ¼" (6-mm) brass threaded rod, cut to 10" (25 cm) (see project notes)
- 4 (¼" [6-mm]) brass washers
- 2 (¼" [6-mm]) brass nuts
- 10" x 3.8" (25 x 10–cm) open-ended glass cylinder candle hurricane (available on Amazon)
- Pencils, for dispensing

1. Start by creating the top of the dispenser. If necessary, sand the 3½-inch (8.75-cm) and 4-inch (10-cm) wood disks with 220-grit sandpaper to remove any rough edges. Wipe away the dust with a microfiber cloth. Create the top piece of the pencil dispenser by applying wood glue to the 3½-inch (8.75-cm) disk and attaching it to the 4-inch (10-cm) disk. Measure around all the sides with a ruler to confirm that the disks are centered.

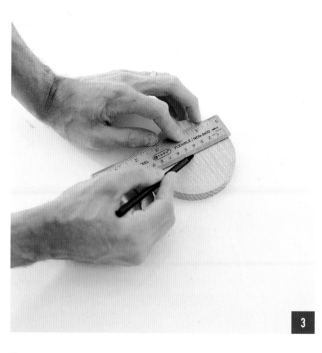

**2.** Hold the disks until the glue sets, allowing it to dry before moving forward.

**3.** With a ruler, measure the center on the attached disks (i.e., the top of the dispenser) and the remaining 3½-inch (8.75-cm) disk (i.e., the bottom of the dispenser). Mark the center with a pencil on both the top and bottom disk.

**4.** Hold the top (attached disks) on a scrap wood block, and drill through the mark created in step 3 with a ¼-inch (6-mm) bit. Repeat this process for the bottom 3½-inch (8.75-cm) disk using a ⅜-inch (9.5-mm) bit.

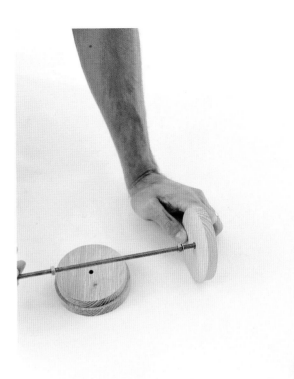

**5.** On the bottom 3½-inch (8.75-cm) disk, insert a brass connector cap through the ⅜-inch (9.5-mm) hole.

**6.** Thread the brass rod through the wood disk and into the connector cap. On the top of the rod, place a brass washer and a brass nut. The washer and nut will be tightened on the bottom disk.

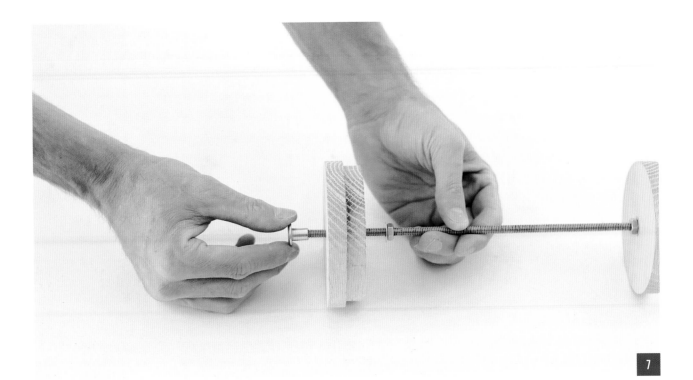

**7.** Thread another washer on the threaded rod, about 1 inch (2.5 cm) from the top. Place a washer on top. Slide the top wood disc on the threaded rod and adjust as needed so that the threaded rod sticks out of the top. On the top, thread and tighten the remaining brass connector cap. Tighten the brass nut under the wood top until it is tight between the nut and connector cap.

**8.** Insert the top-bottom unit into the glass cylinder and fill with pencils. (Tip: Pens or paintbrushes can also be stored in the dispenser.)

### PROJECT NOTES

• Cut your own wood disks or purchase them at your local craft store or online store, such as Etsy.

• The threaded rod can be cut at your local hardware store with a bolt cutter. A zinc threaded rod will also work—simply spray-paint it gold to match.

# WATERCOLOR FABRIC-WRAPPED BOX

Time frame: 2 to 4 hours | Workspace: Medium

We all need to make use of valuable desk or shelving space. One of my all-time favorite ways to do this is with covered boxes. They allow everyday items to be kept in the open yet concealed. Turn them into pieces of art by wrapping them in custom fabric. Source the fabric from your favorite shop, such as Spoonflower or Etsy. Try searching "watercolor fabric" and see what comes up. I love that you can find a hand-created look—without the extra work.

## MATERIALS

- Paper box of choice, packaged flat (IKEA Tjena shown)
- Hair dryer
- Fabric of choice, washed, dried and ironed (yardage per length of fully open box lying flat; 2 yards [1.8 m] shown for 2 boxes; fabric shown sourced from Spoonflower, by designer Trizzuto, design name inhale // exhale)
- Scissors
- 1" or 2" (2.5- or 5-cm) foam brush
- Modge Podge (spray adhesive will also work for most sections)
- Pencil
- Self-healing cutting mat
- X-ACTO knife with #11 blades
- Permanent fabric glue (Aleene's Fast Grab Tacky Glue shown)

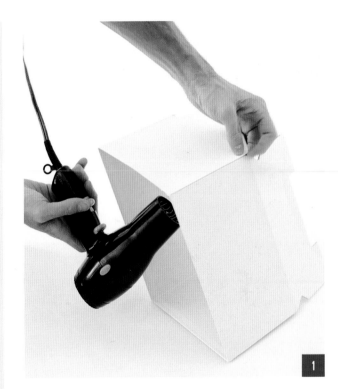

1. Locate the paper seam used to join the box together—it will be a paper flap about ½ inch (13 mm) wide. Run a hair dryer along the seam to loosen the glue. Gently open the seam as the glue loosens. Leave the lid intact.

2

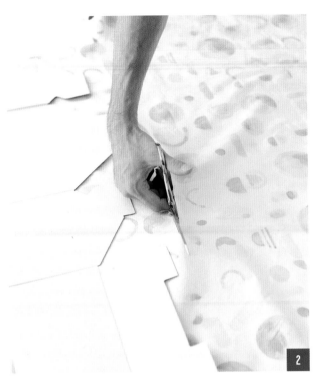

3

4

**2.** Lay the box flat on the fabric, aligned with a straight edge. Leave about 1 inch (2.5 cm) around all the edges. If applicable, confirm that the print is straight. Trim around the box with scissors.

**3.** Ensure that the exterior of the box is facing up. With a foam brush, apply Modge Podge to the exterior of the box. Ensure that the fabric is straight and apply the Modge Podge in about 6-inch (15-cm) sections. Place the fabric on top (with the front of the fabric facing outward).

**4.** Smooth the fabric with your hand as you go. Set the box aside and weigh it down with heavy objects (such as books) while the Modge Podge dries.

**5.** As the bottom of the box dries, place the lid on top of the remaining fabric and allow about 2 inches (5 cm) on all sides. Test the fabric by folding it over the lid's edge and ensure that the fabric completely covers the side and inside edge of the lid.

**6.** With a foam brush, apply Modge Podge to the top of the box.

**7.** With the face of the fabric facing up and ensuring that the fabric is straight, apply it to the lid of the box and smooth the fabric with your hand.

**8**

**9**

**10**

**8.** Once the bottom of the box dries, trim the edges of extra fabric. On the top of the box (the end that the lid fits over) measure ½ inch (13 mm) upward, draw a line with a pencil and trim the fabric with scissors.

**9.** On the self-healing cutting mat, with the inside of the box facing up, trim the sides and bottom flush with the edge of the box with the X-ACTO knife.

**10.** On the top edge of the box, apply Modge Podge ½ inch (13 mm) down and fold the ½-inch (13-mm) flap of fabric down.

**11.** Finish wrapping the box lid. Apply Modge Podge to all edges of the lid and smooth the fabric down, leaving the corners out.

**12.** On the short side of the lid, fold the corner by folding it in (applying a little Modge Podge inside the corner). Then fold the top down, aligning with the corner. Finish the box lid by trimming as necessary and securing with Modge Podge.

**13.** Connect the seam taken apart in step 1. Apply permanent fabric glue. Connect the seam, lay the box flat and weigh it down with a heavy object to dry. Once the glue is dry, assemble the box per the manufacturer's instructions.

# WOOD AND CONCRETE BOOKEND

Time frame: 2 to 4 hours | Workspace: Small

Using simple, contrasting materials provides a striking look. They are also perfect for a small space because they allow books or binders to be organized while still within easy reach. I love the contrast between the warm wood grain and cool concrete. It's one of my favorite combinations!

## MATERIALS

- 2 (3¾" [9.3-cm]) 1 x 6 oak board pieces
- Chop saw (optional)
- Ruler
- Pencil
- Scrap wood block
- Drill with ⅛" (3-mm) countersink bit
- Wood glue
- 4 (1¼" [3-cm]) screws
- Duct tape
- 1 x 4 board, cut to approximately 8" (20 cm)
- 6" (15-cm) clamp
- ¼" (6-mm) plywood, cut into a 4 x 8 rectangle (or 4-mm blank stencil plastic sheet, cut to size), for the concrete mold
- Bagged concrete mix (countertop or low-aggregate mix recommended)
- Bucket
- Trowel

### PROJECT NOTE

The directions for this project involve making a single bookend only. I recommend repeating the steps simultaneously to create the second bookend.

2

1. Cut the oak into 4 (3¾-inch [9.3-cm]) sections with a chop saw or at your local home improvement store.

2. On one end of the oak pieces, measure screw placement with a ruler, ⅜ inch (9.5 mm) from the edge and ¾ inch (19 mm) on both sides. Mark these spots with a pencil. Set aside the 2 oak pieces.

**3.** Place a piece of oak on the scrap wood block. Drill through the marks created in step 2 using a drill fitted with a ⅛-inch (3-mm) countersink bit. Repeat this step with the other piece of oak.

**4.** Apply wood glue on the end of the other piece.

**5.** Attach the 2 oak pieces at the drilled holes. Secure them using 1¼-inch (3-cm) screws.

6

7

**6.** Flip the wood so the inside of the bookend is facing up. Insert 2 (1¼-inch [3-cm]) screws just until the threads grab—do not go all the way through. Measure approximately 1 inch (2.5 cm) from the corner seam. These screws will help support the concrete once it's poured.

**7.** Protect the entire outer surface area of the oak by applying duct tape to all sides. This will prevent discoloration from the concrete seeping.

**8.** Form the mold for the concrete. Apply the 8-inch (20-cm) piece of 1 x 4 board along the open diagonal of the 2 oak attached pieces. It just needs to be a little longer than the diagonal. (Most home improvement stores have small pieces of scrap wood for free.) Connect the 2 pieces by tightening a clamp from the corner of the wood to the 1 x 4 scrap.

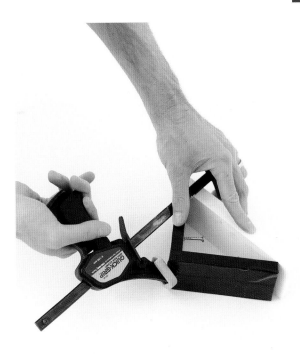

8

**9.** Trace the outline of bookend on the ¼-inch (6-mm) plywood (or stencil film for a no-saw version). Cut out the plywood and place it on the bottom of the bookend. Connect it with duct tape to hold it in place.

**10.** On a flat, level surface, mix the concrete in the bucket per the instructions on the package and fill the bookend mold to the top, using a trowel to help. (Tip: Once the bookend is filled, lightly jiggle the mold. This will bring the water to the top and help smooth out the surface.) Allow the concrete to harden, being sure to wash the concrete tools immediately after using them. Once it hardens, remove the clamp, mold pieces and duct tape and allow it to fully cure, following the manufacturer's instructions.

# CONCRETE AND WOOD DISK LAMP

Time frame: 2 days | Workspace: Medium

In this tutorial, I'll show you how to make a concrete and wood–striped lamp base inspired by high-end designer lamps. The materials are basic, but when they are placed together, they turn into a striking combination.

When considering lighting for your space, have a few layers in each room, such as recessed, chandeliers, sconces and table lighting. Table lights are perfect for creating a cozy look.

## MATERIALS

- 6" (15-cm) round silicone cake mold (see project note)
- Ruler
- Permanent marker
- Bucket
- Bagged concrete mix (countertop or low-aggregate mix recommended)
- Trowel
- 3" (7.5-cm) section of ½" (13-mm) diameter PVC pipe or wooden dowel
- 5 (6" [15-cm] diameter, 1" [2.5-cm] thick) wood disks (oak shown)
- Drill with ½" (13-mm) bit
- Wood glue
- Wood feet for lamp base (¼" x ¾" [6 x 19–mm] flat molding shown)
- Removable tape
- All-purpose construction adhesive for wood and concrete (Liquid Nails shown)
- Lamp kit

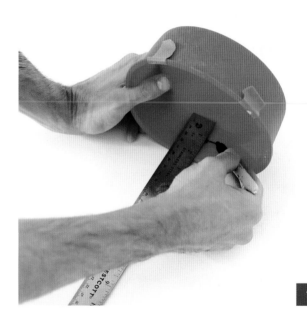

1. Prepare the silicone cake mold by marking 1 inch (2.5 cm) from the bottom on the inside on three sides with a ruler and permanent marker. This will be the height of the concrete disc.

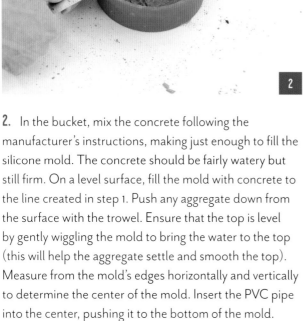

2

3

**2.** In the bucket, mix the concrete following the manufacturer's instructions, making just enough to fill the silicone mold. The concrete should be fairly watery but still firm. On a level surface, fill the mold with concrete to the line created in step 1. Push any aggregate down from the surface with the trowel. Ensure that the top is level by gently wiggling the mold to bring the water to the top (this will help the aggregate settle and smooth the top). Measure from the mold's edges horizontally and vertically to determine the center of the mold. Insert the PVC pipe into the center, pushing it to the bottom of the mold. Wash the concrete tools immediately after using them.

**3.** Once the concrete has set, remove it from the mold and allow it to fully cure on a level surface.

**4.** Repeat steps 2 and 3 if needed to create a total of 5 concrete disks.

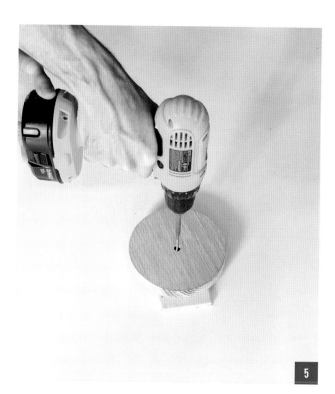

**5.** Measure the center on all the wood disks. Drill a ½-inch (13-mm) hole through all the wood disks.

**6.** Prepare the bottom of the lamp by gluing the wood feet to one of the wood disks. (Tip: Any wood the thickness of the lamp cord or thicker will work.)

**7.** Once the glue securing the lamp feet and base has dried, turn it over so that the feet are sitting on the work surface. Start laying out the lamp, alternating concrete and wood disks. Turn the disks around to test the fit and select the front sides. Mark the fronts with a small piece of removable tape.

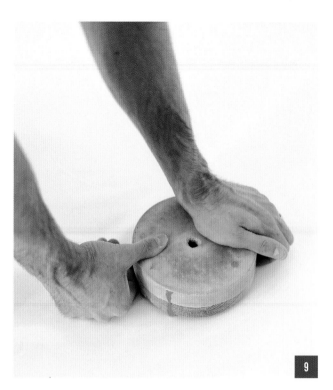

**8.** Start assembling the lamp. Starting on the bottom wood disk, apply construction adhesive to the top. Be careful not to get too close to the edge as it will not dry clear.

**9.** Place a concrete disc on top, line up the tape marks and firmly press down until it holds. With the lamp vertical, continue layering the lamp until the desired height is reached. Allow the construction adhesive to fully cure.

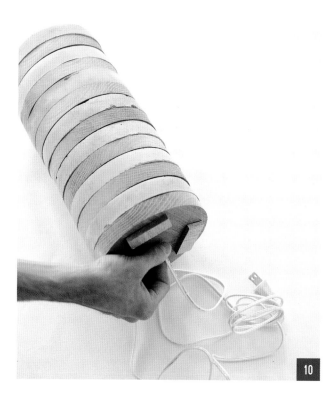

**10.** Once the lamp has completely dried, thread the wire from the lamp kit through the center hole. (Tip: It may be helpful to tape the wire to a thin, straight object to push through the hole.)

**11.** Follow the directions on the lamp kit and wire the lamp. Before securing the top, test the lamp shade height by holding up the shade and adjusting the height as needed.

> **PROJECT NOTE**
>
> Use multiple molds to cast several concrete disks at once, if desired. Mix up enough concrete to fill them all at one time.

# RESOURCES

## ENTRY

Front door—Builder's Choice Elite 4 Lite from The Home Depot (similar styles at Houzz)

Runner—vintage (similar styles at eBay and Etsy)

Snake plant and planter—The Home Depot and Marshalls (similar styles at Target and west elm)

Folding leather bench—DIY, Dorsey Designs

Wall color—Sherwin Williams Pure White

Flooring—Cali Bamboo Shoreline (similar styles at The Home Depot)

## KITCHEN

Cabinets—Welch Maple White Dove by KraftMaid from The Home Depot

Countertop—Snowy Ibiza by Silestone from The Home Depot

Hardware—Square 3¾" (96-mm) Flat Black Liberty Hardware from The Home Depot

Pendants—Brynne by Feiss from The Home Depot

Sconces—Artcraft Jersey 1-Light Vintage Brass Sconce from The Home Depot

Floating shelving—DIY, Dorsey Designs

Appliances—Samsung from The Home Depot

Stools—Pincross counter stool from west elm (similar styles at The Home Depot and Target)

Countertop planters—HomeGoods (similar styles at Target)

Wood cutting boards—The Home Depot (similar styles at Target)

Runner—Safavieh Natural Kilim Gray from The Home Depot (similar styles at Target and HomeGoods)

Wall color—Sherwin Williams Pure White

## DINING

Rug—Unique Loom Monaco from The Home Depot (similar styles at Wayfair and Overstock)

Dining chairs—Safavieh Bandelier from The Home Depot (similar styles at Wayfair)

Folding leather bench—DIY, Dorsey Designs (similar styles at Serena & Lily and Etsy)

Wallpaper—Brume Sky from Stagg Design Shop (similar styles at Rebecca Atwood and Spoonflower)

Vases—Target (similar styles at Wayfair and HomeGoods)

Wall color—Sherwin Williams Pure White

Flooring—Cali Bamboo Shoreline (similar styles at The Home Depot)

## LIVING

Sectional—Harmony from west elm (similar models at Homesense and Wayfair)

Rug—Zarina from World Market (similar styles at Homesense and HomeGoods)

Black and white tassel throw—Heddle & Lamm (similar styles at Etsy)

Geometric panel wall—DIY, Dorsey Designs

Art—Beach print, David Pascolla, Agave and City prints, Juniper's Print Shop, printed through Mpix (similar services at SnapBox and Snapfish)

Pillows—Danielle Oakey Shop and Stagg Design Shop, Leather Circle Pillow (page 25)

Glass vase—Hearth & Hand from Target (similar styles at HomeGoods)

Plaid vases—Target (similar styles at HomeGoods)

Snake plant and planter—The Home Depot and Marshalls (similar styles at Target and west elm)

Wall color—Sherwin Williams Repose Gray

Flooring—Cali Bamboo Shoreline (similar styles at The Home Depot)

## BEDROOM

Bed—DIY, Dorsey Designs

Pillows—Gage from Danielle Oakey Shop (similar styles at Motif Pillows and HomeGoods)

Duvet cover—Roar+Rabbit Circle Lattice from west elm (similar styles at Crane & Canopy and Target)

Rug—Souk from west elm (similar styles at Homesense and HomeGoods)

Rattan stool—HomeGoods (similar styles at Wayfair)

Succulent planter—Marshalls (similar styles at Homesense and HomeGoods)

Vase—Target (similar styles at Homesense and HomeGoods)

Brass shell dish—vintage (similar styles at Etsy)

Drapery—Ritva gray at IKEA (similar styles at Wayfair and HomeGoods)

Wall color—Sherwin Williams Pure White

## WORKSPACE

Desk—vintage (similar styles at west elm and Wayfair)

Rattan desk chair—vintage (similar styles at west elm and Wayfair)

Desk chairs—Safavieh Bandelier from The Home Depot (similar styles at Wayfair)

Lounge chair—vintage Eames (similar styles at Design Within Reach)

Tassel throw—Kate Spade from HomeGoods (similar styles at Target and Wayfair)

Hanging chair—Serena & Lily (similar styles at Pier One and HomeGoods)

Fiddle tree—The Home Depot

Paper and wire vase—Taylor's Eclectic (similar styles from Etsy)

Wood vases—Target (similar styles from Wayfair)

Wood circle art—DIY, Dorsey Designs

Art—Beach print, David Pascolla, Splash print, Juniper's Print Shop, printed through Mpix (similar services at SnapBox and Snapfish)

Wall color—Sherwin Williams Pure White

# ACKNOWLEDGMENTS

Early on, after starting the blog on a whim, I casually thought about writing a book. Readers would occasionally suggest it. So if you've ever sent me a word of encouragement, thank you! It really means more than you know. Thanks so much to all the friends that I have made through blogging. You've given me motivation to keep going. Your support really means so so much. I love the community that I've found through blogging!

Thank you to our family. Now that we are parents, we understand the sacrifice, unending love and support it takes to be parents. And we truly have the best parents. Thank you to my parents for encouraging me and pushing me to reach my full potential. Thank you for always being willing to help watch John and help get project supplies. To David's parents, thank you for frequently helping behind the scenes on many, many projects around the house and watching John with such love and enthusiasm.

Thank you to Page Street Publishing, and especially Sarah Monroe and Meg Palmer. You have been such a joy to work with. I knew working on this book while John was under a year old would be a stretch, but I decided to do it because it was such a good fit. Thank you for the push to get started and the constant support along the way, making this such a seamless process.

# ABOUT THE AUTHOR

Sarah Dorsey is the author of the DIY and interior design blog Dorsey Designs (www. dorseydesigns.com), where she has shared her journey to make small rentals into homes. Together with her husband, she cocreates DIY projects for the home. After living in seven small rentals in nine years, she believes that you don't have to have a large space to feel at home.

With a background in fine art and interior design, Sarah has been creating since she was a young child. She has an undergraduate degree in fine arts, focusing on painting, and a graduate degree in interior design.

Sarah has been featured on several online platforms, such as Design*Sponge, Apartment Therapy, HGTV, The Home Depot, Oprah.com, west elm, CNN, Bob Vila and Pottery Barn. She has also been featured in printed publications, including *Better Homes and Gardens*, *Do It Yourself* magazine, *HGTV Magazine*, *Make It Over Magazine*, the west elm catalog and *Redbook* magazine. She has been a contributing writer for Houzz and eHow.

# INDEX